Praise for Michael Furie's
Spellcasting for Beginners:

"Michael Furie brings fantastical stories about magic and spells back to reality with this dedicated work aimed at those embarking on the long journey into magical practice."

—Raymond Buckland, author of
Buckland's Complete Book of Witchcraft

"A comprehensive and indispensable guide to the basics of practical magic. It is truly a treasure trove of information and advice thoughtfully designed to benefit the novice spellcaster."

—Gerina Dunwich, author of *Wicca Craft,*
Exploring Spellcraft, and *A Witch's Halloween*

SUPERMARKET MAGIC

About the Author

Michael Furie (Northern California) has been a practicing witch for more than fourteen years. He began studying witchcraft at age twelve, and at age seventeen officially took the oaths of the Craft. An American Witch, he practices in the Irish tradition and is a priest of the Cailleach.

To Write to the Author

If you wish to contact the author or would like more information about this book, please write to the author in care of Llewellyn Worldwide, and we will forward your request. Both the author and publisher appreciate hearing from you and learning of your enjoyment of this book and how it has helped you. Llewellyn Worldwide cannot guarantee that every letter written to the author can be answered, but all will be forwarded. Please write to:

Michael Furie
⁒ Llewellyn Worldwide
2143 Wooddale Drive
Woodbury, MN 55125-2989

Please enclose a self-addressed stamped envelope for reply, or $1.00 to cover costs. If outside the USA, enclose an international postal reply coupon.

Creating Spells, Brews, Potions & Powders
from Everyday Ingredients

SUPERMARKET MAGIC

MICHAEL FURIE

Llewellyn Publications
Woodbury, Minnesota

First Edition
First Printing, 2013

Book design by Bob Gaul
Cover design by Adrienne Zimiga
Cover illustration by Anne Wertheim
Editing by Laura Graves
Pentagram art by Llewellyn art department

Llewellyn Publications is a registered trademark of Llewellyn Worldwide Ltd.

Library of Congress Cataloging-in-Publication Data
Furie, Michael, 1978–
   Supermarket magic: creating spells, brews, potions & powders from everyday ingredients/Michael Furie.—First Edition.
      pages cm
   Includes bibliographical references.
   ISBN 978-0-7387-3655-6
   1. Magic. I. Title.
   BF1611.F87 2013
   133.4'4—dc23
                          2013033384

Llewellyn Publications
A Division of Llewellyn Worldwide Ltd.
2143 Wooddale Drive
Woodbury, MN 55125-2989
www.llewellyn.com

Printed in the United States of America

Contents

SECTION 1

SHOPPING AND THE WITCH

Introduction

I get out of the car, find a shopping cart (hopefully one without a squeaky, wobbly wheel), and walk into the grocery store with only one thing on my mind: magic! I know that sounds like a silly notion, but it really isn't. A grocery store is a great place to find a wide variety of ingredients for powerful spells. Herbs, spices, oils, foods, and drinks are all gathered in one easily accessible place; no searching out expensive, odd ingredients in various occult shops or traipsing through the woods desperately trying to find the correct root, herb, or fungus. You have literally thousands of magical ingredients at your disposal without any of the hassle of trying to obtain them individually from various sources. Much has been written in the past about herb magic and some things have been written about food magic, but precious little has been written about how to work powerful magic with ingredients exclusively from the supermarket.

Magic, in order to continue to be relevant in our lives, must evolve and grow as we do, and also as our culture grows, changes, and expands. The supermarket, then, being our modern marketplace and (almost) apothecary, offers us a fantastic and ample supply of items to use in magic, to the exclusion of difficult-to-obtain and exotic ingredients. No longer should anyone feel forced to sift through endless mail-order, Internet, and catalog sources searching for just the right herb or oil when such a wealth of magical supplies exists so close to our own homes. The possibilities are practically limitless.

I spent some time toying with what to call this book. Some other possible title ideas were *I Can't Find Weird Ingredients, HELP!*, *I Live With People and I Don't Want Them to Know I Do Magic*, and *I Can't Afford All the Fancy Stuff, Help!* Any of these names would be appropriate for this book because it covers a wide variety of ingredients, ideas, and spells you can perform at home after a quick trip to your local supermarket to pick up all the necessary items. These spells are modern and will require no complex preparation or ingredients, nor will there be any grand, overly involved rituals needed.

I prefer a simple approach in all I do. Witchcraft is drawn from the magic of the common folk; not the wealthy aristocracy. Most witches of the past were never able to afford brass hanging censers, copper pentacle platters, and ritual swords; they used what they had. In keeping with that spirit, we should use what we have available to us: a large variety of herbs, oils, candles, and foods at our local markets. Not that fancy or expensive tools and ingredients are bad, far from it; it's just that they are sometimes difficult to find and of course they *are* expensive. When I was first starting out, I used a kitchen knife as an athame and pretty much only worked with herbs, oils, and candles I could buy at the supermarket. I lived in a small town where exotic herbs were impossible to get, and there weren't any occult supply stores within at least fifty miles, so except for the few herbs I was able to mail-order, the local grocery store was my witch shop. A handmade wax pentacle, a chalice I was lucky to find at a thrift store, my kitchen athame, a stick for a wand, a clay cauldron-shaped pot my mother gave me, and ingredients from the supermarket made up my entire collection of witch supplies—and they worked very well. To this day, oregano is my favorite magical herb.

If you are already an experienced witch or magical practitioner, I hope this book will add to your practice, but if you have never cast a spell, chapters 2 and 3 focus on explaining all the basics of magic and spell casting, making this a complete volume of both theory and practice. The book is broken down by intention, and for each magical intention several options are given. This type of magic could be described as kitchen witchery since it is a rather "use what is available and what works" approach to casting spells. While it is worthwhile to invest your time in the acquisition of specific ingredients, and definitely worth the trouble of making candles or performing full scale rituals, it is not always possible to do so. In that case we need simple, effective spells that can be used whenever needed.

CHAPTER 1

For Better or Worse: Navigating the Supermarket

When I was a kid, I loved to go shopping. Of course, when you are a child, things often seem a lot more adventurous than they really are. As an adult, grocery shopping is usually a weekly two- to three-hour ordeal for me, as I have to stop at four different stores to gather all the essentials. As a witch, being around large groups of people can be a bit of an emotional minefield; all those people, most of whom are hurriedly searching for their needed items, just fill me with anxiety. I have made the mistake of going to a supermarket on the day before Thanksgiving twice in my life, and it has become a goal of mine to never, ever do that again. That crowd was just unbearable!

Despite some flaws, such as crowds or narrow aisles, supermarkets can be wonderful treasure troves of magical ingredients. They have herbs, candles, oils, food and drink, things like cheesecloth which can be used for charm bags, and sometimes even incense sticks or oil diffusers, which bring added magical atmosphere. Properly prepared, a witch can have a calm, pleasant shopping trip and load up on all sorts of magical essentials. Granted, some stores are larger than others and to get all the ingredients for a spell may take more than one stop, but none of the spells included here contain any overly exotic or rare ingredients. Of course, if you live near one of those mega markets, everything will probably be right there.

The first time I walked into one of those gigantic, warehouse-type supermarkets I was genuinely awe-struck; I could not believe how many different products were all brought together in one place. Granted, the place was about the size of a football field and they were loading crates of food onto the shelves using an actual forklift, but it was still all in one building. Personally, I feel that the rise of the mega warehouse supermarket is a mixed blessing. While it is wonderful to be able to buy such an incredible variety of food in one place, having to work our way through over a hundred people just to get a bag of potatoes, a box of cereal, and some yogurt is a huge drawback. Luckily, there are still smaller "mom and pop" markets out there, and the energy in many of them is so much softer. They are usually much easier to shop in and what they may lack in variety, they more than make up for in relaxed atmospheres. Of course, if you're like me and you have to do weekly grocery shopping at the big stores for your family, it is a good idea to have a magical game plan to help insulate you from some of the potential frenzy.

Witches are by nature psychically sensitive people and though this has many spiritual advantages, our sensitivity can make it difficult to handle being in large crowds. Most of the witches I know avoid large groups of people for this reason, which can make grocery shopping in megamart-type stores exceedingly stressful. For me at least, establishing a bit of a routine is helpful, as is shopping in off hours. I always write my shopping lists the night before I intend to go to the store, and I try to write down the items in the order I find them in the store. I've been in there so many times, I can picture the layout in my head as I make the list. The first time I went to a store and almost no one was there was an amazing experience. The huge supermarkets here are open twenty-four hours a day, and I ended up having to buy a few things at eleven o'clock at night. I walked into the store and it was like a ghost town. It was so quiet and empty. The only people in the whole store were the employees stocking the shelves. It's a fun experience to shop in a giant supermarket when it's practically empty. For safety's sake, it makes more sense to shop in early morning off-hours, like with the small breakfast crowd from 6am to about 9am, than it does to shop around midnight or later, but either way, the stores are usually much less crowded.

When the stores aren't full of people it is so much easier to shop slowly and browse. That's when you can find all sorts of new things to try. I had never tried quinoa until just last year, and I love it; I happened to find it in the store one day when it wasn't too crowded and I was able to look around for a while. Grocery shopping can actually be a lot of fun if you have the time and there aren't a ton of people in the store. I don't mean to imply that people are bad or that when shopping in a large crowd, the people will be mean or anything. I'm just saying that a significant portion of the stress many people feel when grocery shopping stems from the glut of psychic energy around large groups of people. Witches and psychics tend to feel this discordant energy more than the average person.

Being a realistic person with a hectic schedule, most of the time I end up having to shop during the busy hours. I figure that most of us are in the same crowded-supermarket-stress situation. That being the case, a good defense against the psychic pandemonium is shielding. In my book *Spellcasting for Beginners* there's a spell in the "Verbal Magic" chapter for creating a psychic shield of protection. I include it here, as it is a good idea to surround yourself with a magical safeguard to help block all that chaos, if there is any. This spell should be cast before you head to the supermarket.

Protection

If you feel in need of protection, visualize yourself surrounded by a bubble of white light that condenses and "solidifies" into a shining, mirrored orb that repels any and all negativity and danger. As you visualize, chant the following:

> *Shield of power, protect me from harm,*
> *From threat of danger, negativity, and storm;*
> *Glowing power, mirrored might,*
> *Keep me safe with your magic light.*

This spell really does help, though it may have to be repeated more than once if the crowds are too big. The last time I went shopping, the store was packed, so I had to repeat the spell silently to myself four times as I went through the aisles.

Another similar spell to help the overall shopping experience is something I like to call an Anti-Anxiety Orb. This spell is for those times when you forget to work a protection shield before you go into the store and the anxiety has already crept in. Like the standard shield above, it can be repeated and strengthened as needed.

Anti-Anxiety Orb

Find a place to stop for a moment and imagine a thin thread of cool, electric-blue light coming down from above and entering your body through the top of your head. Imagine this thread continues straight through the middle of your body, down to your feet. Now, imagine that the thread is expanding within you and pushing out all the stress and anxiety. See this light expanding until it has become an orb around you and you are fully cleansed of the anxiety and protected from any further psychic disruption. To seal the spell, say this chant to yourself:

> *Anxiety banished, stress cast away;*
> *Calm returns, here to stay.*

The key to this is starting with the thinnest thread so that as it expands it pushes out all the anxiety, leaving you calm and refreshed. I love this spell and use it often.

For help in casting these two spells, please see the next section. It covers all the steps in casting spells, such as meditation, visualization, projection, timing, colors, ethical considerations, etc., and should give you a solid grounding in magical philosophy. If however you are already magically experienced, you may want to skip ahead to section 3 or just skim the next two chapters. Personally, I like to review the basics in books, both with a critical eye and also to see other people's take on the subject of spell casting. It always gives me food for thought, and it never hurts to brush up on the fundamentals.

SECTION 2

·················

MAGICAL FUNDAMENTALS

There are a number of skills and techniques that every spell caster should know and hopefully master in order to perform successful magic. Meditation and the proper channeling of emotional energy are the most important skills to learn, and this section will guide you through all of the exercises needed to become a proficient magical practitioner of this or any system of practical magic. In addition to the proper training of the mind, it is important to understand that as you send forth the energy of your spell, it radiates out into both the physical plane and the astral plane as a means of manifesting your goal. The physical plane is of course made up of the physical world, and in this world everything emits an energy pattern of its own.

CHAPTER 2

Magical Basics

Mundane Considerations

First of all, make sure that the phone is off and that you are not expecting company. Make sure that you are not overly hungry, thirsty, or having to go to the bathroom. Additionally, it is a very good idea to keep a magical journal or notebook in which you record each spell you cast, the date of casting, the type of spell it is, the moon phase, and (later) the date on which the goal manifests itself. You can also include any personal thoughts you have about the magic, of course. It is not a good idea to let others read your magical journal; keep it personal. Also, never speak of your magic to anyone before your goal manifests, as this can cause problems. Other people's energy can sometimes hinder you.

If there is an abundance of energy contrary to your individual magical goal, then the current of your spell can be hindered and your results will be less effective than they could be, at best. If however you work with the energy currents of the physical world and match the rhythms of your intent to the rhythms of the earth and the moon, your magic will be enhanced instead of hindered. This is the basis for magical timing: to understand the natural currents of the world and to time your spells to coincide with the proper flow of worldly energy in order to manifest your magical goal.

Timing

The simplest form of magical timing is to cast your spell during the proper phase of the moon for your magical intention. The waxing moon (from new to full) is the time for positive, growth-related magic. The three days of the full moon are best for blessings, calling upon Goddess energy, and high energy (large-scale change) spells. The waning moon (after the full moon all the way to the new moon) is the time to cast spells involving release, banishing, and dissolution. More on this in chapter 3.

It is also best—but not totally necessary—to cast your spell during the correct season to enhance its effects. Spring would correspond to the new moon, summer the full moon, autumn corresponds to the waning moon, and winter to the dark moon (the three days right before the new moon). So, for example, the best time to cast a spell to banish a bad habit would be during the waning moon during the season of autumn. This would maximize your ability to connect your intention to the proper flow of energy.

That being said, it is not always possible (or advisable) to wait until the ideal season to cast a spell. Timing your rites according to the movements of the moon is sufficient. If, for example, you've been meaning to quit smoking or something similar, and you want to use magic as an aid, *and* it happens to be October, you have the best conditions in which to work your spell. A dark moon in winter, on the other hand, would be the ideal time to banish unwelcome entities or harmful people, to send them permanently away from you. The darkest time (of both the moon and season) would maximize your banishing abilities. Don't worry though, that type of magic is almost never needed. I'm not trying to scare anybody, I swear.

Another effective means of magical timing is to work according to the days of the week. Each day of the week has specific planetary and magical associations attached to it.

Monday: The day of the moon. An excellent day for psychic and dream work and connecting to goddess energy.

Tuesday: The day of Mars. A great day for any work involving conflict, force, male energy, and action.

Wednesday: The day of Mercury. A day for communication, divination, learning, and mental improvement.

Thursday: The day of Jupiter. The best day to work for expansion, influencing people in positions of authority, and good luck.

Friday: The day of Venus. The ideal day for love, beauty, and friendship magic.

Saturday: The day of Saturn. The day for binding and grounding magic.

Sunday: The day of the sun. The best time for connecting to god energy, success and wealth magic, strength, and healing.

Magical timing is only the first step in the spell casting process. Determining the spell you want to use, and gathering all the necessary ingredients and supplies for it are the next steps.

Supplies

To create some of the recipes in this book, such as the oils, you will need basic cooking items such as a pot, a spoon, a sieve (preferably a metal one), and jars with tight-fitting lids. Some of the spells in this book call for a cloth charm bag. These are not usually available in supermarkets, but a lot of the larger food/pharmacy/automotive/housewares/everything-type stores also have a fabric section. All you need is a 3- to 6-inch square of fabric in the chosen color and some thread, yarn, or cord to tie it up. Barring that, any of the charm bags called for in the spells can be substituted with plain cheesecloth, which is widely available in most regular supermarkets.

You will probably notice that I have not included any incense recipes in this book. The reason for this is that I really wanted the scope of this work to be limited to magical items that could be made and used with only ingredients obtained from the supermarket. Many kinds of incense must be burned on special charcoal blocks. Also, a lot of markets sell prepackaged stick and cone incense that can be purchased in a compatible scent and used in conjunction with a given spell as desired. Lastly, if you would prefer to make your own incense, you can craft your own recipe out of the ingredient listings given at the end of each chapter, or you can modify an oil recipe (omitting the oil and other wet ingredients) from this book to suit your needs. The spells included weren't designed for use with incense, but it can always be included if desired.

When gathering such ingredients as candles and fabric, the color chosen can be an important factor. Color can play an important role in helping to keep all the energies of your spell in alignment.

Colors of Magic

In many spells, you will need to work with items such as candles, cloths, threads, etc. of various colors in order to further focus your intent and charge your spell with added power. The following comprehensive list of colors and their traditional magical meanings can help you select candles and other items that have the type of energy you seek.

Colors and Their Uses

Black: drawing in energy, dissolving illness or negativity, protection, multipurpose

White: sending out energy, purification, protection, air

Red: fire, strength, passion, courage, luck, protection

Orange: communication, energy, change in accordance with will

Yellow: intellect, divination, learning, persuasion, air; clear bright yellow can substitute for gold

Green: growth, fertility, abundance, luck, love (color of Venus), plants, earth

Blue: water, healing, happiness, peace

Indigo: psychic ability

Violet: spirituality, meditation, higher power

Brown: earth, animals

Gray: neutrality, stalemate; clear light gray can substitute for silver

Silver: Goddess energy, dreams, moon magic, intuition

Gold: God energy, strength, sun magic, success, prosperity

Copper: love (due to its association with Venus), beauty

Pink: love, friendship, emotional healing

Once you have all the ingredients gathered together, the next step in the process is spiritual preparation. A disciplined mind is the key to being spiritually prepared. An easy way (no, really!) to condition the mind for magic is through the art of meditation.

Meditation

Meditation is a focusing of the mind and creating within it a relaxed state of awareness. When you learn to properly meditate, you actually alter how your brain functions—lowering the brainwave frequency into what has been termed "alpha" brainwave level. It is this relaxed level of consciousness that is needed when working magic. During a proper meditation designed to create a magical mental state, a person is able to shift consciousness at will and use the "alpha" level to harness, program, and project magical energy in spellwork.

You needn't worry that the alpha level is unnatural or permanent. We all enter this state whenever we feel sleepy or our attention remains relaxed for at least three minutes. It is very common to slip into alpha level while watching television, for example. As soon as you shift focus, your brain returns to the "beta" level, the higher rate of waking consciousness. It would be pretty hard to cast a spell while watching television, not to mention while sleeping. This is why meditation is so necessary. We can use this process to shift our mind into a magical state and still keep our focused awareness. This is vital to our successful use of spellcraft.

Now that you know the reason behind the use of meditation in spellwork, the question then becomes, "How should I *actually* meditate for magic?" First, you find the time to meditate. Now, I am not saying that you need to find an hour a day to meditate or any other such nonsense, I'm merely saying that you should meditate at least once a day, even if it's only for five minutes or so. Meditating frequently and for longer periods of time would condition the mind faster, but any amount of conditioning is a step in the right direction. You needn't feel inferior by anyone saying that you need to meditate for X amount of time or in such-and-such a fashion in order to do it "correctly." There is no single way to properly meditate for magic. Many paths lead to the calm center.

Here's a quick sample meditation for you to use in order to move your mind into an alpha brainwave state easily. You can record yourself reading the meditation aloud and play it back as a guide, if desired.

The Autumn Tree Meditation

Sit in a comfortable position, preferably in a chair with your back straight and eyes closed. Take three slow deep breaths; in through your nose and out through your mouth. Next, form a mental picture of a small tree (about four feet tall) with only three large branches. On the first branch see three large leaves, on the second branch see two large leaves, and on the last branch see two more large leaves, for a total of seven leaves on the tree. At the base of the tree notice a small hollow with a soft glow coming from within the tree.

Since it is autumn (in the meditation), a soft breeze begins to blow and it brings your attention back to the softly waving leaves. You gaze at the first leaf and see it turn a beautiful shade of red and fall off the tree, caught in the breeze. You look at the next leaf and see it turn an autumn orange, get swept up in the breeze and carried away. You see the third leaf turn yellow and flap in the breeze until it too is taken from the tree. Now, focus on the fourth leaf. It is still green but its strength is fading, and it too is taken by the breeze. See the next leaf turn a strangely bright shade of blue as it detaches from the tree branch and drifts off into the cool air. The sixth leaf darkens into a deep midnight blue and crumbles into the air. Finally, move to the last leaf on the tree. It has turned a lovely sunset purple. You decide to reach out and pluck this leaf.

You hold this leaf in your left hand, and as you clutch it, you notice that the tree seems to be getting bigger. You quickly realize that the tree is not changing; it is you who is growing smaller, shrinking down to about three inches in height. The purple leaf has transformed you into just the right height to go into the hollow of the tree. You step into the hollow and find a staircase. Walk slowly down the ten steps of the staircase. When you reach the bottom, a door appears before you…

This ends the structured part of the meditation. Where you go from here is your choice. At this point you are in an altered state of consciousness and can either continue on with the meditation and go through the door, or you can use this "alpha" level to work magic. If you choose to work magic, follow the example instructions given in the Spellwork Sequence that follows.

There are many other mediations you could use to achieve the proper altered state of consciousness, although some may be less direct in their approach. Some may be geared specifically toward journey work, in which you mentally travel to another place, or they may be designed for pathworking, a guided meditation in which you are led to an inner revelation. Whatever your magical goal, this meditation is an ideal starting place for spellwork. Before casting a spell, simply use the meditation to get in the proper frame of mind. Once you are in the alpha state, your next move should be to properly focus your intent. This is accomplished through uniting the three aspects of the personality: thinking, feeling, and willing. Let's examine thinking first.

Thinking

Thinking and rational perception come from the left side of the brain and are usually the first part of the spell casting process; we contemplate the rational elements of our spell. When trying to create change through magic, it is best to get a clear mental idea of what you want to happen, the end result of your spell: your goal. As a general rule, do not envision the process of attaining this goal. Don't focus on how something *should* happen. Focus only on the end result. If you get too caught up in the process, you slow down the achievement of your goals and alter your success.

A secret to successful magic is to have clear intention. This intention should be simultaneously general and specific. Confusing, aren't I? What I mean by this is that you need to have a specific *type* of goal in mind, such as "I want the correct love in my life," while still keeping the overall details of the goal general, as opposed to "I want [insert name here] to fall in love with me." You can make a list of attributes you would like the proper love (in this case) to possess and focus on those specific qualities without naming a specific person, but be aware that this would somewhat slow the process. The more conditions you place on a spell, the longer it takes to manifest. It is best to keep your mind focused on your goal and that the goal itself be as general as possible while still meeting your specific need.

Properly focusing our thoughts is only the first step in the process of creating the correct magical mindset. The next step is to take time to examine your emotions regarding the magical goal.

Feeling

The aspect of feeling is extremely important in working magic. It is an aspect that is often underrated and downplayed. Too often magical practitioners cast a spell while filled with desperation or fear and then wonder why the results of their spell fail to manifest or manifest in unpleasant or inadequate ways. Improperly focused feeling is a major cause of unsuccessful magic. The need for the aspect of feeling and emotion is often mistakenly taught as a need for belief. In truth, you do not have to "believe" in magic in order for it to work any more than you would have to believe in electricity to watch television. If one is properly trained and casts a spell with the proper focus, it will manifest. That reality can almost be a hindrance if your spell isn't infused with the correct emotion.

When I was a kid and new to the Craft, I was unaware of the need to infuse how you wanted to feel into the spell you are casting. I was more into learning by trial and error than by the loving guidance of those with more experience. The problem was that at the time, I could only cast a successful spell when I was totally desperate; it was the only time I could feel and move the energy needed for magic. This of course resulted in spells that were successful, but the results left me feeling even more desperate than before. Keep in mind that this was very early in my magic workings, and at the time I had almost no knowledge of mind conditioning or energy work...and really had no business casting spells in the first place! I just wasn't ready yet. But, I digress. It is precisely because of my early unfortunate experiences that I must adamantly stress the importance of proper feeling. It is my intent to help as many people as possible avoid making that magical mistake.

A better approach to feeling is to focus on how you will feel when your goal is reached. Feel the happiness, calm, joy, relief, or whatever you would like to feel when the magic manifests. This creates that feeling as a condition for your spell, which is a good magical safeguard against unforeseen problems. As an example, if you cast a money spell and are filled with fear because you really need the money, that fear will be infused into your spell—either the money won't manifest as needed (thus fulfilling your fear) or it will manifest in a way that makes you feel fearful (such as an accident settlement). A safer option is to focus your feelings on a calm sense of security, in which your needs are met, and also on the joy you want to feel when your goal manifests. This way, the feelings of joy and security are infused into your spell, resulting in a much better overall outcome. Another magical safeguard is to cast a spell with the intent that the spell be "with harm to none" and/or "for the good of all." When you add either or both of these conditions into your spell it greatly reduces the risk of a spell causing negative side effects. See chapter 3 for more details on this.

As much as I carry on about the importance of feeling, it is not the only other important thing, of course. Let us now move on to the power and importance of will.

Willing

The power of the human will is of incredible importance in magic working. When you are filled with clear intent and positive emotion, and add the fierce conviction of your will—the drive to *create* change as opposed to merely influencing it—you have a recipe for magical excellence. Your willpower comes into play as the catalyst for the transmission of the energy. Your willpower fuels your ability to project energy (which will be covered next) and is key to activating the spell. Thinking programs the spell, feeling energizes the spell, and willing activates the spell and readies your intention for projection. If you do not have the willpower, the intention, the desire to *create* change, you will not be able to work magic.

Now, let me give you an example. Let's say that you are casting a spell to gain employment. By *creating* change, as opposed to requesting change or attracting change, I don't mean (necessarily) that you should believe that you are zapping up a job—you are not creating a job. That's not what I mean. You are holding the job in place for yourself (in the future) in linear time. What you are creating is a series of changes: altering future possibility, bending it in your favor (first spiritually, then physically) in order to develop and encounter the *opportunity* to get a new job. The position may seem to "fall in your lap," but you didn't create the job itself (usually; there are exceptions to everything); you created a ripple in the water. The momentum of the ripple created a wave, the wave reached the opposite shore (your goal), and, as waves do, it doubled back in your direction with your opportunity floating on its surface. You created the ripple *and* the opportunity. Please forgive the drawn-out metaphor. I am trying to illustrate the proper mindset you need to have in order to reach your magical goals. You need to have an understanding that in magic, you are not really working with just the "law of attraction"; you are also working with your innate ability to create.

If you are focused only on drawing things to you, you are creating an unconscious perception of deprivation. This perception of deprivation creeps into your spell. A feeling of lack can be ruinous to any magical activity. This is a secret that many neo-witches aren't being taught, sadly. In order to *properly* work the magic, you need to cultivate an understanding that you have the power of creation inside of you; from that which has created you, you can in turn, create. We are all manifestations of energy from our creator (many witches call her the Great Mother). In science, we are taught that energy itself cannot be created or destroyed; it merely changes form. Thus, assuming that our level of scientific understanding holds up throughout the cosmos, the energy that the Goddess/God/Creator/Great Spirit used to create everything (including us) was part of Her/His/Its/Their own energy, their own being. This means that everything in the universe is connected to the creator and also to each other, having all been created from the same source. It also means that we have a similar (though lesser, of course) capacity for creation. We create everyday. We create through our intent, through our desire, and through our actions—thinking, feeling, and willing, respectively.

We are beings that are creative by nature. We were given life by a creative entity and we, in turn, have the ability to create. This is what we have to keep in mind in order to properly work magic: We can create! This is the source of your willpower. This is your strength. This is not delusion or ego, because it is balanced by the fact that all beings possess this same ability. This is the plain and simple spiritual truth. Now that thought (intent), feeling (desire), and will (the drive to create) have been united, all that is left is to project it out into the cosmos to bring it into manifestation. But how do you project it outward?

Projection

There are different ways to project the energy of the spell. Some of the methods of projection are built right into a given spell. If you are using or making a focus for your spell (poppet, talisman, candle, etc.), the charging of that focus is a means of projecting the energy of the spell. For example, in a candle spell when you charge the candle, you are projecting the energy into the candle and it is released when you burn the candle. The basic method for projecting energy is:

1. The shifting of your consciousness;

2. The unification of thinking, feeling, and willing;

3. The element of directed visualization.

Doesn't that sound easy? Heck no? Well, it sounds a lot more complicated than it is.

Firstly, the shifting of consciousness is just getting into the alpha brainwave state; it's just magical meditation. Secondly, uniting thinking, feeling, and willing is how you program your spell. Finally, directed visualization is just fancy jargon for using your imagination in a conscious way. At the proper point of the spell, all you have to do is visualize the energy streaming from your third eye and the palms of your hands, either into the object you are charging or out toward the target of your spell. Specifically, you actually need to imagine the energy leaving you and reaching your goal at its location, or see it reaching a symbol of your goal, such as a candle or charm. This is how you program your subconscious to do the work. The subconscious works with images—shape and color. You connect your conscious mind to your subconscious mind through mental imagery, your imagination. Seriously, that's it. The secret to actually making magic work is the combination of all these steps. If you just visualize your goal without shifting into an alpha brainwave state, you will not be able to move the energy as successfully. If you shift into alpha and visualize without having the will to create or adding any emotional connection to your goal, you will not be able to successfully move the energy. The secret is the combination—you need all of it for magic. That's the secret *and* the truth.

Spellwork Sequence

Here is a summary of how to use each of the steps in order to work a spell of any kind. Afterwards, I will follow up with a basic charging rite for creating a talisman or magically loading a candle. Let's examine the complete process. As an example, say we want to cast a spell to gain money. What do we do?

We start by determining the correct moon phase for the intended goal of your spell. In this case, we are looking to increase our money so we need to work during the waxing phase. We could also time our spell by the day of the week and work on a Sunday for wealth and success. We need to think about why we desire more money. The motivation behind our desire must be thoroughly contemplated and understood. In this case, let us say that the motivation is too many bills and a need to have more money to make ends meet. Once the motivation is understood, we need to reduce it down to a precise goal (clear intent) and a goal that is for the good of all, with harm to none, its (the goal's) equivalent or better. (More on the reason for this in the next section.)

To reach our clear intent where money is concerned, we need to figure out how much money we need right now. So we should look at our bills and expenses and determine how much more money we need to meet those expenses, versus the amount of money we have or will make at that time. Let's say that our clear intent is this: We need at least $251 more, according to free will, with harm to none, and for the good of all. Okay, we have clear intent for what we need. Now, we move on to the third step. We decide what spell we want to use and make sure we've got all the ingredients necessary. For the sake of simplicity, let's go with a basic candle spell.

For the spell, you'll need a green or gold candle, (green for abundance or gold for success; for more, see Colors of Magic on page 21); Basic Money Oil (prepared in advance; recipe given later, see page 156); a piece of blank, unlined paper; a heatproof dish for burning (optional); and a pen.

After you have gathered your spell ingredients, it is time for the fourth step: meditation. After placing the spell ingredients on an altar table, sit before it. Then go into your meditative state, and once arriving at the door in your imagination (if using the Autumn Tree meditation), open the door and see a blank screen inside. On this screen, an image may come into view like when watching a movie. See yourself on the screen holding two one-hundred dollar bills, a fifty dollar bill, and a one dollar bill; the goal, $251. After letting the image fade, you may see the bills that need to be paid come up on the screen and see a huge "PAID" stamp on each one.

Now, consider how you will *feel* when your bills are paid. Feel the relief wash over you. Bask in this feeling. Let this feeling inspire you to succeed. Build the will to manifest your goal. Feel yourself creating the magical energy to bring you money (what happens is that you create a change in your personal energy and make it "hum" at the abundance frequency). Now, pick up the green or gold candle, hold it firmly in your dominant hand, and mentally send your energy into the candle. You are charging the candle with your thought (visualization), emotion (feeling), and will power (energy). Send it all into the candle mentally. Next, anoint the candle with the money oil. Anoint it from the middle to the top and again from the middle to the bottom, as if you are filling it with power (which you possess and are doing). Now pick up the pen and paper and write a rhyming chant including your goal (a spell). For the sake of example, I have one prepared:

> *Bills unpaid, looming threat;*
> *I need some help, relief from debt;*
> *$251.00 my goal,*
> *With harm to none, for good of all.*
> *Bills are paid, joy is here;*
> *Money woes disappeared!*

You have two choices when you cast this spell: burn the paper in the candle flame (which means you will need a heatproof dish to set it in), or place the paper beneath the candle and once the spell has been cast, fold the paper up and keep it in your wallet until the goal has manifested. If you choose to burn the paper, it is a good idea to copy the chant down in your magical journal along with all of the other pertinent information. After you have written the spell on the paper, charge the paper in the same manner you charged the candle; holding it in your dominant hand. When this is done, either place the paper underneath the candle (if you are saving the paper) or set it in front of the candle (if you are going to burn it). If you are going to burn the paper, light the candle and then say the spell while you burn the paper. If you are going to keep the paper, say the spell as you light the candle. Either way, summon all your focus and intent, and as you say the spell, "breathe out" the magic—take a full inhalation and speak the spell and with the exhalation; mentally send the power out into the cosmos.

Finally, clap your hands together once to affirm that it is done.

Once the spell has been cast, you can either leave the candle to burn out if it is safe to do so (this is best), or you can extinguish the candle with a candle snuffer or the back of a spoon. Don't blow it out, it scatters the energy. Finally, if you have kept the paper, fold the paper into a small square by folding each corner to the middle, toward you, as many times as you feel necessary to make it small enough to carry with you. If you have chosen to burn the paper, bury the ashes outdoors. The spell is complete.

The next step is of course to wait for your goal to manifest. This can happen in several ways: you could receive money that had been delayed, you could win some money, you could get a raise in pay or some sort of gift, or you could receive several different small financial gains that "just happened to" add up to be exactly what you need.

Write down your results in your magical journal. Give any spell that you cast a minimum of a full lunar cycle (28 days) to begin to manifest. During this time, it is okay to work additional magic toward the same goal to act as a booster. Some spells manifest very quickly, while others take longer. Because it varies, it's important to keep track!

There are a lot of choices in the magical arena. You can pick and choose which methods work best for you; keep track of what works for you personally and what doesn't.

Charging Ritual

This ritual is all-purpose and can be used to charge anything with magical energy. The charging will need to be done according to an appropriate moon phase for the type of charge desired. Once you have selected the item—be it charm, talisman, candle, statue, or whatever—you have to clean it. Ideally you should run it under clean, cold water, but that is not always possible. If you have to dust it instead, that's fine. Just do what you can. Afterwards, set up an altar (any small table will do) with the following items:

- A cup of saltwater

- An appropriately colored candle

- The tool, item, or object to be charged

Procedure

Gather all the tools and items necessary and arrange the altar. Next, go into a meditation and reflect on what your goal for the ritual is, i.e., the type of charge you want the item to hold. The next step is to begin the rite.

Settle yourself before the altar and hold the item to be charged in your hands (if the item is too large, place it on the altar and hold your hands above it). Close your eyes and see the item in your mind, while at the same time sweeping your dominant hand over the item in your other hand or on the altar. Say, "I neutralize energy not in harmony with me and fill you with [intention] power! For the good of all and by land, sky, and sea; as I will, so shall it be!"

Repeat this chant three times and pass the item over the candle flame and sprinkle it with saltwater. The charge has been made. The rite can now be concluded. Wrap the charged item in natural cloth of appropriate colors until you use it in a spell. This keeps the item clean, safe, and fully charged until needed.

CHAPTER 3

Magical Ethics

When You Should,
When You Shouldn't ... And Why Not!

There are several "rules" and laws regarding the ethical use of magic and these rules are followed for a variety of reasons; personal safety being among them. Some of these rules include:

- Any spell you cast should be cast with the intention that it shall be according to free will and for the good of all.

- Magic should not be done (solely) for personal gain.

- What you send out returns to you.

- Work according to the moon phases.

All of these magical laws have been found to be useful and correct, and they are all intertwined. They have been followed for untold generations in one form or another by magically minded people. Let's briefly examine each of these rules individually and detail why they are necessary.

Let's start with the first one: Any spell you cast should be cast with the intention that it shall be "according to free will and for the good of all." Why? Well, if you send all your magic out with the intention that it be for the good of all, you *never* ever have to worry about unforeseen negative consequences from accidental, irresponsible, or so-called black magic. Any spell you cast with the intention of "for the good of all" already has a built-in safety net to prevent any and all controlling or cursing elements of a spell from manifesting in the first place, thus saving you from having to endure the consequences. The "according to free will" part also ensures the safety and responsibility of our magic by focusing within our intention the condition that our spells will not coerce, compel, or control the free will of another in order to manifest our magical goal. Witches are taught the concept of Infinity of Solution, the belief that no one needs to suffer in order for our happiness to exist; everyone can win; we can all be happy at the same time with harm to no one. This belief has been reinforced through our life experiences and our magical practice. If you use magic to reach your goals according to free will and for the good of all, you ensure that your work is positive, progressive, effective, and most of all, proper.

The second reason it is advised you do your magic according to free will and for the good of all is a bit more selfish (but that's okay). The reason is that when you work your magic in this way, you virtually ensure your success. You automatically maneuver around the obstacles and opposition that would exist out there in the universe to a magical goal that was sent out in the spirit of "I want this no matter who gets hurt or what the cost." That attitude would not be conducive to successful magic since everything and everyone is spiritually interconnected; many destinies are intertwined with one another. If you cast a spell for something you desire no matter what, then if you are powerful enough to get it, you have caused a disruption in the flow of events for both yourself and others who are connected to you. If you work for the good of all, you are not creating a disruption; rather, you are merely adding your specific desire *into* the flow of current events. With this one subtle act you make a profound difference. You remove opposition, you create rather than disrupt and/or destroy, you nurture rather than neglect, and you empower rather than weaken everyone involved. Now unfortunately, this doesn't mean that as long as you work in this way you will never have a magical failure; you still might, but the scales of success versus failure will be greatly tipped in favor of success.

The second magical rule is: no magic should be done solely for personal gain. This rule should be taken with a grain of salt. It goes along with the previous rule, that magic should be done for the good of all. There is nothing wrong (thank goodness!) with using magic to get what you want. Granted, magic is a spiritual practice and is a byproduct of our spiritual learning and understanding. It can seem irreverent or even sacrilegious to use this energy and knowledge for the acquisition of mundane things, but it needn't be. Magic is a gift, and this gift is meant to be used for the betterment of our lives and the lives of those around us (assuming they desire it). Confusing, aren't I? I tell you to not use magic for personal gain, imply that it is a sacrilege, and then say to go do it. My guideline for this is that if your desire or goal will better your life and enhance who you are (or the one asking for the goal), then the use of magic is not only okay but also highly encouraged. If your goal is frivolous (a spell for a new car is important; a spell just to get a "better" car than a next door neighbor is not) or harmful, I would advise against using magic to achieve your goal. Using magic for personal gain is only bad or incorrect if you use it for frivolous ends or in such a way as to cause harm. That's it, case closed.

The next rule regarding magic is that what you send out returns to you. This rule is not just magical; it permeates every aspect of our lives. Everything we do creates a ripple effect, since we are connected to one another and to the universe in which we exist. Everything that exists vibrates at a certain pitch. Everything is particle *and* wave. It all interacts and intermingles and affects itself and each other. When you drop a stone into a pond, it creates ripples in the water that radiate out to the edge and then double back to the point of origin. The waves ALWAYS return to the point of origin (granted, frequently they return in a weakened or subtle state). It is the same with our actions. Our actions generate a spiral of energy that reaches first outward, then inward, back to the point of origin. This is why we should always conduct ourselves in a positive manner. The physical nature of the earthly plane is slanted toward decay. As living beings, we have the responsibility to create, maintain, and foster growth. If our actions are positive and nurturing, positivity and nurturing energy will be released and (eventually...) return to us in the form of positive and nurturing life experiences. This is not to say that bad things won't ever happen to good people—I am merely saying that through positive thought, action, magic, and experience you will tip the scales in favor of an overall happier life for both yourself and others.

Some say that what you send out returns threefold, others say that it returns to you tenfold, and still even others say it returns in equal proportion or, like ripples in a pond, in a weakened or relaxed state. Either way, know that it does indeed return, and you are much better off making sure to conduct yourself in such a manner that it does not return with a vengeance.

Your experience may vary as may your life choices, but I shall end this subject on a personal note: When I was young(er) and stupid, I misused magic for petty revenge once. Without going into detail, let's just say what goes around came back around to me and I haven't misused magic since. Don't say I didn't properly warn you!

The final general magical rule that I will discuss is one that can be found in virtually any magical guide (including earlier in this one): time your work according to the moon phases. The reason for this rule is that the moon exerts a great deal of influence upon humans, animals, plants, and the earth and ocean. This influence is due to the moon's gravity, light, and, in its orbit, the angle at which it resides in relation to both the earth and sun. When the moon is new, it is lined up with the sun; a perfect alignment would be a solar eclipse. This is considered to be a powerful time; the reason for this is that the gravity of the moon and the gravity of the sun have a similar influence on our bodies, since the moon is small and close and the sun is huge, but really far away. When they are in the same general area in the sky, we are being "pulled upward" as I like to say, by both at the same time.

The moon is waxing after the new moon until the full moon (approximately fourteen days). During this time, the moon appears to be moving away from the sun and growing in light. As such, the gravitational influence of the sun and moon is gradually separating instead of being jointly focused on us like a laser beam. The waxing phase of the moon is an excellent and much preferred time to work magic toward positive, growth-oriented goals such as increasing abundance, finding love, gaining luck; indeed, gaining anything. If you are looking to increase and/or gain, the waxing moon is the right time to use magic toward your goal. It is the active springlike/summerlike time of the lunar cycle.

The moon is full when it is on the opposite side of the earth from the sun. The side we see is fully engulfed in sunlight and appears to our eye to be complete in its roundness. This time in the lunar cycle is very powerful and can be difficult if you do not proceed with caution in your endeavors both magical and mundane. The reason being is that gravity from the moon is pulling us in one direction and the sun is pulling us in the opposite direction, so to speak. You may know that the word "lunacy" is a term originally used to denote the weirdness that can overtake some people at this time, and indeed, some people do act rather loony for the three days of the full moon. It can also be a difficult time for people who suffer from migraine headaches, as these tend to be worse during the full moon time for many sufferers. I would venture to guess that is due to the gravitational pull from both the sun and moon acting on us from opposite directions. That being said, when we are in the middle of the alignment of earth, moon, and sun, we are opened up psychically to a much greater degree of magical energy and spiritual awareness. If we make use of our access to this "magical boost," we can work very powerful magic during this phase. During the full moon, it is best to work magic toward psychic awareness, Goddess worship and understanding, physical and spiritual protection, divination, and anything having to do with the "infinity of solution." So if you are embroiled in conflict and need to find a way to make everyone happy, now would be the time, but if you go the peacemaking route, release all expectation of what you want to happen beforehand to avoid unfair manipulation. This time in the lunar cycle is delicate and powerful and should not be taken lightly; it should be respected and used only for important goals. That helps take away any possibility of lunacy... thank goodness!

The waning moon is after the full moon up to the new moon, when the moon appears to be moving toward the sun and decreasing in light. At this time, our bodies are readjusting from the gravitational force of the full moon and preparing for the gravitational focus and new beginning of the new moon. During the waning moon our bodies and minds are in release mode, so it is best to work magic to release, remove, and rid oneself of anything harmful or unnecessary. It is an ideal time for banishing, healings (in the form of casting out illness as opposed to building strength), curse removal, and deep spiritual grounding and centering. It is also a good time for introspection, reflection, and meditation—any task involving turning inward. This can be a dangerous time since we are a bit more open and vulnerable to the energies around us. This is the time in the lunar cycle that some foolishly work dark magic against others, regardless of consequence. Since we are of a magical mindset and therefore more open than most people, I would suggest the wearing of protective amulets at this time to ensure that others' negativity does not find its way to you. Also, I would like to add a warning that when working magic to rid oneself of obstacles or block-ages, be specific. If you are too general and cast a spell to remove all your obstacles, things may leave your life that you would rather keep—jobs, friends, a spouse, etc.—and while these changes may be for your ultimate betterment, you may not wish for them to go so quickly, all at once, and without warning. As a rule of thumb, when working magic to gain something, be general. When working magic to remove something, be specific.

Aside from any of these magical rules, the basic ethic that has been more or less followed is: do what you want as long as it does not hurt yourself or anyone else. Many will recognize this as the Wiccan Rede: An it harm none, do as you will. As long as we remember to not allow ourselves to be harmed by others, this is a fine magical guideline.

SECTION 3

....

SUPERMARKET SPELLBOOK

We now come to the meat and potatoes of this book. My impetus for writing this book was the need for a practical working manual for modern magic that does not contain the hard-to-find exotic ingredients which are quite unavailable or surprisingly expensive for most of us. Given the vast amount of herbs, spices, oils, vinegars, and foods that are readily accessible to us, I felt it was time to thoroughly tap into it. Please note that although there will be foods and some food recipes listed in this section, this is not a cookbook.

In this section, we will be primarily focused on magical ingredients with recipes for oils, vinegars, potions, etc., and of course spells in which to use them. I've divided the spellbook into sections based on magical desire and since herbs are versatile, you may see the same ingredient listed in more than one section. To help avoid confusion, I have included an herbal index at the back of the book with every ingredient from each section listed in alphabetical order.

Before we get to the individual spells and recipes, I would like to go through the steps involved in the making of the oils, potions, powders, vinegars, etc. First, let's look at the making of magical oils.

Preparing Magical Oils

To begin, gather your herbal ingredients, a pot, and the chosen oil together along with a spoon, strainer, and a bottle for the completed mixture. Break up the herbs with your fingers and hold each individual herb in your hands and make clear your intention for the finished oil you are making. This will charge the herb in your hands, readying it for the oil. Do this with each herb. Hold it in your hand, focus on your intent, and sprinkle that herb into the pot. When all the herbs are in the pot, pour the proper amount of the oil (amounts are given in each recipe) over them and swirl the pot to blend the mixture. Next, warm the oil over *very* low heat, stirring slowly but constantly until you can smell the scent of the herbs in the air. This will let you know that the essential properties of the herbs have been transferred to the oil. Remove the oil from heat and allow it to cool. When it has cooled, strain the oil into a jar, and charge the completed mixture using the Charging Ritual given in chapter 2.

The above general procedure should be followed for all the oil blends found within this book. It is a simple and enjoyable process, but if you live with people who are not magically minded, you can always say that you are experimenting with making your own flavored cooking oils, since these blends are made from edible ingredients from the supermarket. This *only* works with the oils presented in this book as I have written them. No modifications should be made, and you will still have to worry about food allergies if you choose to consume any of the formulas in this or any book. I wouldn't recommend consuming magical oils anyway; aside from any inherent danger, these recipes are not designed for taste, but for magical energy. They may taste really gross depending on the ingredients.

Preparing Potions

This is an incredibly easy process, and you may even use a coffee maker to make these if you desire. All you have to do is hold the individual herbs or tea bag in your hands and charge them as stated previously in the instructions on preparing magical oil. Put your ingredients in a pot (a cauldron is ideal) or in a coffee filter you can pop into your coffee maker. Next, pour in the necessary amount of water and simmer over low heat (or turn on the coffee maker) for about ten minutes until bubbles form at the bottom of the pot (or until the coffee maker is finished brewing) and steam is rising, but do not let the water boil. Boiling the water is only necessary in the case of extracting the essence from tough roots and will not be used in the recipes presented here. To boil these potions would damage the essences we are trying to extract and use. After about ten minutes, remove the potion from heat or turn off the coffee maker, cover, and allow to cool for ten to fifteen minutes. When cooled, strain and sweeten if desired. The potion is ready to use.

Preparing Powders

This is the easiest task of them all. All you have to do is grind and charge each individual herb by hand and place it in a small bowl with the required amount of cornstarch. When all the herbs have been added, mix them together with your fingers, charge the completed powder, and bottle for use.

Preparing Vinegars

This process is basically the same as making a potion with two VERY IMPORTANT exceptions: (1) Do not use your coffee maker, and (2) Don't use an iron pot or cauldron—it will rust! You only need to heat up the herb/ vinegar mixture for about five minutes, then cool, strain, bottle, and charge. I warn you: making vinegars is not the sweetest-smelling process. You can also go the longer route of just bottling the chosen herbs and vinegar without heating it and allow it to sit for about a week to extract the herbs' essences. This is a less involved process and produces a good result; it just takes longer.

Now that we've covered the basics, let's move on to the fun stuff. Each of the following chapters will be self-contained for their given purpose, detailing all the ingredients, recipes, and spells for the magical goal. Magic is such a personal and versatile process that we often develop our own individual specialties such as using oils, candle magic, or charm-making to the exclusion of other ways of working.

My personal preference is to use candle magic as a first resort, as it is the most natural for me. From there, I like to expand and supplement that work with other methods only if needed, but to each their own. You may find that some practices are more effective for you than others due to the personal nature of this work. Trial and error is the only way to discover this. Most of us, however, find that we can shift from one way to another with a similar success rate, we just prefer one or two methods over the rest. No judgments or guilt should be made about this; instead, our individuality should be celebrated.

Since it is very true that if your life and home are too cluttered, nothing else can get done very well, I have chosen to begin with the chapter on clearing.

CHAPTER 4

Clearing
(and Cleansing)

This chapter focuses on magically clearing both life and home of negativity and strife. All too often we are subject to the turmoil generated by other people's negativity. We may not be able to cast them out of our lives but we can do the next best thing—cast out their negativity and replace it with calm, relaxing, clear energy.

Before we get to the magical means of removing negativity, let's go over energy's basic nature, both positive and negative, and how it is transformed. It is said that energy cannot be created nor destroyed, it only changes form. This is understood in both the scientific and spiritual communities. Magically speaking, we have the ability to summon, focus, "program," project, and/or banish (send away) energy, but no one has the ability to destroy it. Energy is timeless and eternal.

Since we can program or color energy, either purposely with our intent or accidentally through strong blasts of emotion, we have the ability to extract that "coloring" from the energy, though we cannot (nor should we want to) destroy the energy itself. This is how we remove negativity—we consciously focus our intent to transform the energy in the area from negative to positive. This action, in actuality, extracts the negative color of the energy and replaces it with positivity through the projection of our will. This is the basic truth behind any method of energy work; the energy itself is a constant, the intent it carries is all that has changed. Thus, I use the term "negativity" as opposed to "negative energy," since we aren't removing the energy entirely, only the negative programming it carries.

Don't get me wrong—we can send the energy itself away if we choose to, but I personally feel it is far more responsible in most cases to strip it of its vibe/coloring/ charge/ intent/program (so many words that mean the same thing), and reprogram it rather than cast it away as is—filled with negativity only to land somewhere else and create turmoil wherever it winds up. Remember: for the good of all and with harm to none!

There are several different methods to magically clear a space of negativity that you can perform using ingredients from a supermarket. You can sprinkle powders, use floor washes, anoint with magical oils, burn candles, and even make magical charms that will absorb the negativity from the energy. We will examine all of these methods. First I will give the recipes, and then I will follow with the spells. *Note*: All these clearing and cleansing spells are best performed during the time of the waning moon.

Brews

There are many things we can brew together in order to cleanse and drive away negativity; some can be drunk, but others cannot. I will definitely note which is which. Brews created with the intention of drinking them are known as potions and will be listed as such in this book. The first magical brew I will present is the famous Four Thieves' Vinegar, whose origins can be traced back to the Middle Ages. This vinegar is used for a variety of purposes from driving away illness to banishing (or even cursing) other people. There are many recipe variations; some including inedible ingredients such as wormwood, but this is my favorite recipe. Best of all, it contains only easily found and edible ingredients.

Four Thieves' Vinegar

2 cups apple cider vinegar

9 cloves of garlic

1 tablespoon black pepper

1 tablespoon cayenne pepper

1 tablespoon sage

1 tablespoon thyme

Dice the garlic and add it and the herbs into your vinegar. Warm it in a pot (ideally, a glass or enamel pot; no cast iron) according to the basic directions given at the beginning of section 3, and then cool and bottle for four days, keeping it in a cool, dark place. On the fourth day, strain the herbs and garlic out of the liquid, and rebottle the liquid for use. Since it is vinegar-based, it should keep for ages. This vinegar is not meant to be in food, but since it is made with only edible ingredients, it *could* be used in cooking, though I couldn't comment on the taste or any recipe ideas. It could be added in minute amounts to foods as an illness banisher, if you wish to do so. I was told that if you swap out the black pepper and cayenne pepper with herbs such as rosemary and parsley, it would be good to use in a vinaigrette on salads, which I am going to try.

Four Thieves' Vinegar Spells

To use Four Thieves' Vinegar to clear your home of negativity, you can place a small bowl of the vinegar in each room of your home overnight to absorb that negativity. I warn you though, your whole house will smell gross that night and for a while afterward. This ritual is not recommended unless you have a *lot* of negativity to remove. Also, given the fact that you may be the only magically-minded person in a home shared with others, this ritual may be totally unworkable.

You can also use Four Thieves' Vinegar as a floor wash to rid your home of any "astral buildup" or negativity. To do this, simply add a cup of the vinegar to a bucket of wash water and mop or scrub your floors with intent. This is a good way to cleanse your kitchen.

A much less overt, drastic, difficult, and/or stinky technique for ridding your home of negativity using Four Thieves' Vinegar involves a bit of subtle candle magic. Take a white candle and a black candle and anoint them with the vinegar. If you can only find white candles at the store it's okay. Light the candles, preferably in the center of the home or say, as dinner candles on the table. Try to leave the candles lit for an hour or more, if possible. This will burn away negativity and cleanse your home. You can repeat this process once a month if desired, preferably during the waning moon.

Here's a classic method for removing a negative person (an enemy) from your life. This must *only* be done with careful consideration of magical ethics, and this spell should be cast with the intent of "according to free will and for the good of all." This spell permanently removes someone from your life and makes them leave.

Take a square of fresh new paper and black ink. Write the name of the intended target in the middle of the paper and fold it, making the folds away from you so the person's name is covered and cannot be seen. Charge this paper with your intent for the person to leave your life forever, according to free will and for the good of all. Place the paper in a bottle filled with the vinegar. Seal the bottle and throw it in a moving body of water, such as a river or stream. It is done.

A bit of an alternative would be to soak the paper in the vinegar, allow it to dry for a day, and burn it in the light of a black candle, setting it in a heatproof dish to burn to ash. Then, flush the ashes along with the remaining vinegar down the toilet while screaming in your mind:

Leave now, leave me be;
Vile wretch, be gone from me!
By free will, for good of all,
Away from me you shall now fall!

Another useful brew would be a magical cleansing brew, which has multiple uses. Sprinkle it around the home to remove any negative vibrations, cleanse magical tools, or even drink it to cleanse yourself of negativity.

Cleansing Brew

1 tablespoon peppermint
(or a peppermint tea bag)

1 tablespoon thyme

Sprig of fresh rosemary (optional)

1 cup lemon juice

½ cup of water

In a small pot, pour the water and simmer the herbs over low heat for a few minutes until you have extracted the herbs' essence into the water. Remove from heat and add the lemon juice. If you intend on making this an edible cleansing potion, you would be much better off making basic, real lemonade with real lemons and sugar to your taste, and then adding the liquid brewed from the water and herbs into the lemonade. Adding the sprig of rosemary directly into the pitcher of lemonade would be ideal. Whatever you decide to do, charge the brew or potion for the intention of cleansing and use as desired.

CLEANSING BREW SPELLS

As stated earlier, a good technique for using the Cleansing Brew is to sprinkle it around your home to cleanse it. This can be done using the sprig of rosemary as an aspergillum to sprinkle drops of the brew in the corners of each room of your home. You could also use this brew as a floor wash as stated earlier with the Four Thieves' Vinegar recipe. Simply add a cup of the brew to your wash water and scrub or mop the floor with the intent of cleansing held in your mind.

A great method of cleansing your body of negativity is to add the brew to your bath water and take a nice, relaxing, cleansing bath. It is best to fill the bath with only warm (not hot) water and also add a handful of salt to the tub. Once the tub is full, pour in the entire amount of the brew and step into the bath. Relax in the bath for as long as you desire, and when you are ready to get out, pull the plug and let the water completely drain out while you are still in the tub. Feel all the negativity being pulled out of your aura and sucked down the drain. Afterward, you can quickly shower off any residual energy or brew and dry off.

In order to cleanse magical tools, amulets, or any item in need of psychic cleansing of unknown energies, you can simply rub, dip, or wash them with the brew. Just first be sure that the item in question won't be ruined by the brew's ingredients.

Oils

The beauty of using magical oils to cleanse or for any purpose is in their ability to impart within their user the deep power of their intention while being subtle all the while. We can just dab a bit on our wrists, third eye, and the back of our necks (wiping off any excess) and we are magically infused throughout our day without having to carry around bulky crystals, charm bags, or odd-looking jewelry (not that I am opposed to jewelry). Even if you decide to wear your usual cologne or perfume, you can always dab on a bit of oil and its magic will still work for you and not be diluted by the other scents. This is because the *energy* will remain the same even if the scent is overpowered by something else. Using magical oils in cleansing is a very simple and versatile method of removing any negativity from yourself or most environments or objects. There are several ways to use oils to cleanse. The following recipe is a very strong purification/unhexing/cleansing blend that should be used in any of the cleansing spells when you feel really bogged down with negativity or when you feel you may have been the victim of an actual curse (which is exceedingly rare), or even the unintentional blast of negativity we are subject to from others' greed, envy, or anger.

Super Cleansing Oil

   3 bay leaves

   ¼ teaspoon cumin

   ¼ teaspoon chili pepper

   ¼ cup torn onion skins

   ¼ teaspoon grated horseradish

   ½ cup vegetable oil

   Prepare this in the usual manner but be careful: these ingredients are strong and spicy! As for the onion skins, just use the outer skin of the onion so as to avoid the strong onion smell while still preserving the cleansing energy.

Regular Cleansing Oil

This recipe is gentler and can be used for general day-to-day cleansing to keep yourself energized and free of negativity. This oil would also be good for daily use if you are like me and suffer from/are gifted with psi-empathy; it keeps the residue of other people's emotional energy from building up in your psyche and causing needless stress.

½ teaspoon anise

1 tablespoon lemon peel

½ teaspoon basil

1 teaspoon peppermint

½ cup olive oil

Prepare this in the usual way, and use it in your regular cleansings. If need be, you may substitute vegetable oil for the olive oil, but know that the olive oil is included here to lend its peaceful and blessing qualities. Try to include it if at all possible.

Cleansing Oil Spells

A wonderful spell to cast in order to cleanse a home of negativity is to take a white taper candle, anoint it with cleansing oil (regular if it's a general cleansing, super if the need is great) from the middle of the candle out toward the ends, and secure the candle in a sturdy holder. Visualize your intent: see your home bright and free of any darkness. Next, go to the central room in your home (not necessarily the architectural center, but wherever you feel the "heart" of the home is), and light the candle. Now, working in a clockwise direction throughout the building, go from room to room and circle (clockwise!) each room with the candle while visualizing its flame burning away any negative power out of the room's energy. While you are encircling each room, say the following chant to focus your intent:

Darkness break and burn away,
Candle's flame, cleanse this space.
I bless my home and self this day,
Filled with light; gloom erased!

When you have finished encircling each room, go back to the central room and set the candle in a safe place (if possible, if not then extinguish with a candle snuffer or spoon) and allow it to burn out on its own. Once it is fully spent, bury the remains of the candle and wash the candle holder. Repeat as desired, though a monthly cleanse is ideal.

A method of cleansing an object is to first physically cleanse it by whatever method is appropriate and then anoint it with the cleansing oil (if it is safe to do so) while visualizing the object being filled with white light that casts out and dissolves any negative energy contained in the object. Afterward, it is good to gently breathe on the object to infuse it with your own personal energy. This helps repel negativity while simultaneously reconnecting you to the object.

A prime method for cleansing a person of negativity using oil is to anoint them with the cleansing oil on the wrists, third eye, and back of the neck and have them do a grounding meditation such as visualizing all negativity being pulled out of them and taken into the earth to be recycled, leaving them filled only with positivity.

Powders

Magical powders are a good method to cleanse the energy outside of your home and property of negative vibes. It is a good idea to first cleanse before you put up any protections such as shields or wards (see chapter 10 for more information) so that you are not trapping any negativity within the boundary that you create through shielding. To make any kind of powder, you will need to get some cornstarch, and a mortar and pestle or sturdy bowl and the back of a spoon.

Cleansing Powder

1 tablespoon thyme

2 teaspoons cayenne pepper

2 teaspoons turmeric

1 tablespoon cornstarch

Charge each of the herbs with the intent of cleansing and pour each one into the mortar or bowl and then grind them into a powder. Once they are powdered and blended together add the cornstarch and stir. Corn is protective and the starch makes the powder a more uniform texture.

Powder Spells

The easiest (and most obvious) way to use the cleansing powder is to sprinkle it all around the outside of your home and yard in a big circle to cast out any negative buildup in the vicinity. A method of cleansing the inside of your home is one that should be used with caution, depending on what type of floor coverings you have. If you wish, you can sprinkle the powder indoors all around your home and then vacuum it up with the intent that it is removing any negative buildup your home may contain. This method might stain your carpeting, however, so use with caution.

There is a way to use the powder for the cleansing of self. You can transform the powder into a cleansing charm by placing a tablespoon of the powder into a black or white magic bag and tying it shut. Keep the bag with you wherever you go for the entire waning moon phase. If you do not have any black or white fabric handy, you can tie the powder in coffee filters, but it is best not to keep these on your person, as they are fragile and could break. Make several and put one in your car, under your bed, amongst your clothing, wherever you'd like.

Foods

Since food is the fuel the helps your body run, all natural plant-based foods such as grains, beans, fruits, vegetables, nuts, and seeds have a certain amount of cleansing ability. The more processed these foods become, the less cleansing ability they contain. Having said that, there are several food items that can be used to facilitate cleansing of the body, mind and spirit when eaten alone or when used as ingredients in larger meals.

Onions have a particularly strong cleansing ability, and it is believed that whether eaten or rubbed on the body, they have the ability to absorb illness and negativity. Lemons are another strong cleansing food. As previously stated, a properly charged lemonade (again, made by hand from real lemons, not a mix) can be used as an inner cleansing potion. There are several ingredients that, although they do not constitute a meal in and of themselves, will provide a very important boost to meals designed to bring about an inner cleansing from negativity. Such ingredients include parsley, peppermint, rosemary, anise, bay, fennel, horseradish, and potatoes, though the latter food is used more for healing. If you are asking a faery or ancestors for their assistance in cleansing you, then you can add some dairy products to your recipe. Milk, cream, and butter have always been offerings to the Otherworld. Indeed, butter is a symbol of magic and transformation since it has to be transformed from a liquid (cream) to a solid (butter). It has been used for centuries in magic and ritual.

You could make rosemary mashed potatoes with caramelized onions and add milk or cream, some real butter, and charge it for cleansing to make a very potent but modern dish that will feed your body with cleansing energy. You could pair this with lean meat if you wish, but try to avoid red meat as its energy is not conducive to cleansing. If you make gravy for the mashed potatoes, make a mushroom gravy the old fashioned way with real mushrooms; charge it separately also for cleansing. If you wish to add a salad to your cleansing meal (or just make a salad instead) use lettuce, onion, and tomato. Pair it with a lemon vinaigrette dressing.

As you can see, there are a lot of items that may be used to facilitate clearing and cleansing of the body, mind, spirit, and environment of negativity that are very readily available and blessedly inexpensive. In fact, most people have one or two of these items already in their home; all that needs to be done is to properly charge and combine the items and you're ready to go! Depending on what your specific clearing or cleansing goal is, it is wise to make use of as many methods as you feel necessary and are available to you to achieve your goal. For example, let's say you feel tired and bogged down by other people's pessimism and you wish to dissolve it away. If you desire a spiritual cleansing of negativity, you can use Four Thieves' Vinegar in your bath water, anoint yourself with cleansing oils, *and* eat cleansing foods and drink cleansing beverages every day for a week or even an entire waning moon phase if need be. This multi-tiered approach will ensure that you receive a strong and thorough dissolution of that negative psychic grunge, leaving you energized and whole once more. Granted, combining several techniques for one goal is not always feasible, desirable, and indeed not even usually necessary. But if you feel that you need as strong a cleansing as possible, the "use everything" approach is a good way to make sure all points are covered and there are no loose ends.

Shopping List

Here's a short list of the ingredients used in the spells in this chapter for cleansing.

❏ Anise seed	❏ Cream	❏ Onion
❏ Apple cider vinegar	❏ Cumin	❏ Parsley
❏ Bay leaves	❏ Fennel	❏ Peppermint
❏ Basil	❏ Garlic	❏ Potatoes
❏ Black pepper	❏ Horseradish	❏ Rosemary
❏ Butter	❏ Lemon	❏ Sage
❏ Candles (white and black)	❏ Lettuce	❏ Thyme
❏ Cayenne pepper	❏ Milk	❏ Tomato
❏ Chili pepper (dried)	❏ Mushrooms (any edible variety)	❏ Turmeric
❏ Cornstarch	❏ Olive oil	❏ Vegetable oil

CHAPTER 5

Harmony

It is very easy to use magic to bring peace and harmony into your life and home. If you live with other people, you'll have to consider the ethical implications of using magic in your household. I have pondered this myself and come to the conclusion that without another's permission, it is still okay to use magic to surround your environment with a peaceful aura for the good of all. If the other people are then influenced by this energy of peace and harmony, it is according to their own free will, albeit subconsciously. This same idea is true in everyday life: if you were to act positively and optimistically around others and their moods improve as a result, that wouldn't be manipulation—it would be osmosis.

Harmony and peace are gentle. They are the delicate shifting, the "going with the flow" of events as they unfold instead of "fighting the good fight" or trying to be right. Harmony is the calm center, the balance in the middle, and the rejection of living in one extreme or another. Meditation is always a wonderful means of achieving a peaceful, balanced state of being, but it is not always feasible to find the time to meditate in order to feel harmonious in our chaotic world. Luckily, there are numerous simple, effective magical methods to create a more balanced and centered mental state and/or environment.

Brews

Personally, I love brew making; it has always captured my imagination. The idea of standing in front of a fire, stirring a bubbling cauldron filled with a magic elixir, adding unusual ingredients while chanting ancient prayers as the mystic liquid blends together to form a powerful brew is so romantic and alluring to me that I have made brew making an important part of my personal Craft. Granted, I don't create as dramatic a scene as I have just described—usually, my cauldron is on the stove—but the process always gives me a certain sense of satisfaction as well as a useful product.

Brewing a potion for harmony is an easy and useful method of magic that is both subtle and effective. Making a brew to create a feeling of peace and harmony is as easy as grabbing a chamomile tea bag. Chamomile has a soothing effect, and when tea is sweetened with a little honey, it brings about a feeling of peace. You can actually make this potion in your coffee pot by adding the tea bags to the pot and letting them steep in the hot water as it drips into the pot.

Peace and Harmony Brew

> 1 tablespoon chamomile
> (or 2 chamomile tea bags)
>
> 3 cups water
>
> 1 tablespoon honey

You can use the coffee pot method or heat the water in a pot to almost boiling, then remove from heat and allow the tea bags to steep in the water for ten to fifteen minutes. Then pour a cupful and sweeten with the spoonful of honey. Charge the liquid with the intent of peace and relaxation, and take slow sips of the potion. If you intend to use this brew in a nonbeverage manner, omit the honey.

Spells for the Brew

First and foremost, you can drink this brew. It has a wonderfully calming effect. You can also use the unsweetened brew to sprinkle around the house to bring a general sense of harmony in the environment of the home. Another way to use the brew is in a short spell. You can soak a piece of paper in the brew and allow it to dry. Then write your desire for harmony and peace on the paper, and charge it for this purpose. You can then burn the paper in a fireplace or in the flame of a white candle and set it in a fireproof dish to burn to ashes. This way, you will release your intent and cast your spell.

Oils

You can use magical oils to infuse yourself, others, or even objects with a peaceful, harmonious energy. Wearing a peace-inducing oil will help keep you calm in the midst of a chaotic environment. It will also create a gentle and peaceful aura around you that will rub off on others if they subconsciously allow it (no magical coercion intended here), and it will help relax any tension in your surroundings. If you anoint an object with a harmony-drawing oil, you can charge it to be a battery of sorts to radiate a peaceful aura wherever you place it. Once again, I must caution against creating and using magical charms or objects in certain areas of a home (such as their bedrooms, shared with others), unless they have knowledge of it and have given approval.

To set up charms of harmony and/or protection around your own bedroom or in common areas is a fine idea to improve your personal environment, but if you live with others who are unaware of your magical inclinations, it is manipulative to use magic that would affect these other people in their personal areas of the home. You can of course *work* magic that won't affect others in common areas if you need to, only remember that it is bad practice to "use magic on" people without their permission.

Anyway, back to oils. The following recipe is a gentle and effective formula to bring calm energy to you.

Peace and Harmony Oil

1 tablespoon chamomile
(about 2 tea bags' worth)

1 tablespoon dried apple peel

½ cup olive oil

Prepare in the usual way

OIL SPELLS

A wonderful spell for inner peace and harmony is to dab a bit of the Peace and Harmony Oil on your forehead (on your third eye) and take a few deep breaths. Close your eyes and visualize a beam of white light shining down on you, filling your body through your third eye. While the light is filling you, see it gathering up any tension or turmoil in your mind and body. See it being released through your feet into the earth. While you are visualizing, chant to yourself or out loud:

Goddess (or your chosen deity):
Guide my spirit path,
Soothe my soul, protect from wrath.
Grant me mercy, joy, and peace;
My faith in you shall never cease.
Filled with strength from star above;
Bathed in power, light, and love.
Blessed be.

You can relax in this state for as long as you wish. When finished, wipe the oil from your forehead.

Room of Harmony

A good spell to charge a room with the energy of harmony is to take four objects of a similar nature (that symbolize harmony to you) and anoint them with the Peace and Harmony Oil on the base of each object (one at a time) and then hold each object in your hands and focus on the feeling of peace, infusing the feeling of peace into the object. See any incorrect energy being swept away and replaced with the proper peaceful energy. When you have finished doing this with each object, you can place one in each corner of a room so the objects radiate their power into the whole room.

Burn Away the Gloom

To be rid of unpleasant vibrations in a room, take a white candle and anoint it with the Peace and Harmony Oil. Then light the candle and walk the perimeter of the room, holding it up high, burning away the negativity, and replacing it with harmony. You may chant the following as you make your rounds:

Magic flame, burn away the ill,
Clean this space, remove the gloom;
With joy and peace I am filled,
And hereby now charge this room!

You can do this in each room of your home or in one or two rooms as needed. This spell is somewhat of a cleansing, but it also adds the element of charging the room with harmony and peace.

Powders

You can use powders to radiate a gentle aura of peace when sprinkled around the home as a type of potpourri or bundled together as a magic charm. Powders are a very versatile magical product: easy to make, easy to use, and easy to hide if necessary.

Peace and Harmony Powder

    1 tablespoon chamomile

    1 tablespoon grated and dried apple peel

    1 tablespoon cornstarch

Grind the apple peel and chamomile together in a mortar or special bowl you use for grinding, add the cornstarch, and stir. Then charge the powder for peace and harmony. Bottle for use.

Harmony Now! Powder

I have read that of all the zodiac signs, the most stubborn are Aries, Taurus, Leo, Scorpio, and Capricorn. All these signs are in my family, and because of that, sometimes a more potent harmony powder is called for rather than the gentle

Peace and Harmony Powder above. This recipe is not meant to be manipulative, but is strongly solar in influence while still maintaining an overall focus of loving intent. Its goal is to remove negativity while replacing it with loving vibrations to encourage harmony and cooperation—*not* to forcibly compel anyone to get along.

1 tablespoon chamomile

1 tablespoon ginger

1 tablespoon grated orange peel

1 tablespoon cornstarch

First, grate the orange peel and dry it in a warm oven (200 degrees) for a few minutes. Be careful not to burn it. Allow it to cool. Next, place all ingredients except the cornstarch into a mortar and grind them to powder. When the herbs have been powdered, stir in the cornstarch, and charge the mixture for harmony and peace. In your mind's eye, see the power of the powder dissolving any negativity and replacing it with gold-flecked white light wherever it is sprinkled. Feel hopeful, relaxed, and calm as you charge the blend. It is now ready to be used as a body powder, ingredient for a charm bag, or in one of the following spells.

Powder Spells
Peace Potpourri
A good idea to bring peace to a room is to sprinkle either of the powders into a bowl and then place a favorite potpourri

on top of it. The room will smell nice and radiate peaceful energy. This should be replaced monthly.

Plants of Harmony

You can add either of the powders (they aren't poisonous) to the soil of your houseplants to infuse them and the room they are in with harmonious vibrations. I wouldn't use more than a tablespoon of the powder per plant. When you water the plant, the powder will be absorbed into the plant and this will infuse the whole plant with its power. The plant will then become like a magic charm and its aura will radiate enough of the energy to alter the feel of the room.

Foods

Food alters body chemistry. This is a fact. To anyone who doubts this, I would suggest they have three cups of coffee and some chocolate-covered espresso beans, and then see how they feel. As previously stated, the less processed the food is, the better it is for you. Everything you eat is absorbed and/or used by your body in some way. There are many people who have unknown food allergies and they can be unfortunate victims of radical mood shifts due to food-related reactions. This of course would have a negative affect of your sense of peace and harmony. Food is a tricky area, and caution should be used when incorporating it into a magical practice. One person's delicacy is another's hospital stay.

Having said that, there are some foods which are known to induce a more peaceful state of being and a relaxed mind that, unless you are allergic, can be used whenever you wish. My personal favorite is chocolate. Although chocolate is primarily used as an aphrodisiac, it is also an excellent mood-shifting food that brings about relaxation and a sense of peace when used in the proper manner. If you wish to use chocolate, please find the best quality chocolate you can with the highest cacao content (the active ingredient), and use it with a magical intention. Don't just eat a candy bar or drink a mocha while typing (as I am doing right now) and expect much of a change. You might feel a bit better, but a more profound shift will occur if you make your magical use of chocolate into a small ritual.

Secret Potion of Delicate Harmony

What is this mystic secret elixir? It's hot cocoa. Aren't I dramatic? I couldn't help myself! But I'm serious: if you put the proper intention and effort into it, you can turn ordinary hot cocoa into a strong relaxation-inducer. There is a bit of caffeine in chocolate, but it is balanced out by the tryptophan and milk; tryptophan is an amino acid which has an effect of drowsiness and relaxation, since it helps create serotonin and melatonin in the body. Both are natural chemicals that have a calming effect. Like I said before, use the best quality cocoa you can find. If possible, use unsweetened chocolate powder and add sugar on your own. This will create a stronger blend than prepackaged hot cocoa mix.

The most effective method is to charge the chocolate, sugar, and milk separately for relaxation and harmony, then warm the milk on the stove slowly. As the milk is warming, mix the sugar and chocolate together and then gently stir the mixture into the warming milk. I am not going to give precise measurements here; hot cocoa, like coffee, is a highly personal affair where people vary greatly in preference. Some people like it really sweet, some like extra chocolate, and others prefer a thin cocoa. I will leave it to personal preference and experimentation.

After the drink has been prepared, pour it into a favorite mug or cup and take it to a comfortable place you can sit and enjoy the cocoa. It is very helpful while sipping to do a grounding exercise such as visualizing that you grow "roots" into the ground and that all your frustrations and any negativity are pulled out of you through the roots and reabsorbed into the earth.

A "Healthy Food" Alternative for Harmony

If cocoa is not your thing or you simply want another method to create a peaceful state, here is a healthful salad. Lettuce has many relaxing properties. Indeed, the hearts of lettuce are gently sleep-inducing when eaten. The following recipe is a nice blend of flavors that will have a relaxing effect.

HARMONY SALAD

> 1 part romaine lettuce
>
> 1 part iceberg lettuce
>
> 1 part red-leaf lettuce

½ cup grated zucchini

¼ cup cheese of your choice

1 avocado, diced

Shred and mix the lettuce with the zucchini, cheese, and avocado. Top with the following dressing.

Harmony Vinaigrette

3 parts olive oil

1 part apple cider vinegar

2 pinches salt

Dash pepper

Place all ingredients into a jar with a tight-fitting lid and shake all ingredients together until well mixed. Pour over the salad and stir the salad a bit before eating. If desired, you could use some of the Four Thieves' Vinegar from chapter 4 in place of the plain cider vinegar called for in this recipe. Just don't use a store-bought Four Thieves' Vinegar in food, as some have inedible ingredients.

Food is a wonderful means of changing the body and mind, drawing them away from harm and disorder and helping them to return to a state of balance. I love food, and it is one of my favorite methods of creating change. Of all the methods of bringing peace and harmony outlined here, food is the best for inducing a personal inner change. Each of the magical practices presented have their own advantages and disadvantages, and you will probably develop personal affinities for one or two methods over other. Remember that harmony and peace are gentle magical intentions; no force is required. If the environment is too heavy with negativity, you should probably cleanse the area first in order to create a "blank" space that you can then fill with peaceful energy. This will create a stronger sense of peace and harmony.

Shopping List

Here's a list of peace and harmony ingredients to use in the spells and recipes in this chapter.

❏ Apple	❏ Cornstarch	❏ Orange
❏ Apple cider vinegar	❏ Ginger	❏ Pepper (black)
❏ Avocado	❏ Honey	❏ Salt
❏ Chamomile tea	❏ Lettuce (iceberg, red-leaf, and romaine)	❏ Sugar
❏ Cheese	❏ Milk	❏ White candle
❏ Cocoa powder (unsweetened)	❏ Olive oil	❏ Zucchini

CHAPTER 6

Healing

Healing is a fantastic magical practice. It really is awe-inspiring to magically heal someone of illness or speed the healing of injury. The witches' theory of illness is that it is caused by imbalance. This seems to be confirmed to some degree by modern science, since it is now believed that chemical imbalances in the brain can create mental disorders and that other bodily imbalances create blockages, illnesses, and disorders—everything from depression to gall bladder issues to certain cancers, etc. Witches are taught in the practice of magical healing that we are sending energy to heal the astral body, which then filters down to the physical body and helps it to heal itself.

The body alone is an incredibly wonderful organism that continually heals itself everyday. New cells are born every minute; old cells wither, die, and make room for the new. We filter out waste and excess and renew ourselves constantly. When the body is overwhelmed by too great an amount of illness, however, it cannot battle back from it alone and needs our assistance to become whole once more. That's where modern medicine and our own practice of magical healing come in—no matter what practice (modern medicine or healing magic) is employed, it works by empowering the body's own healing abilities to restore itself. Sometimes, in strong cases such as chemotherapy, modern medicine employs destructive means in order to destroy the illness, after which the body is allowed to resume its own restoration process.

For the most part, *magical* healing methods involve only the restorative techniques to allow the body to return to a state of wholeness. These are the ones recommended and practiced by myself and everyone else I know. It must also be stated that magical healing is not a substitute for modern medical attention; each school should be used for their respective good points and also to balance what the other one lacks. Witches do not have a disdain for conventional medicine—we use what works! We use magic and science together with the understanding that magic is a science in itself, and that each is a part of the greater whole. The colors I use in magical healing are white, for universal energy to be sent wherever it needs to go, such as when the actual cause of the illness may be unknown; light blue, for specific healing energy sent to an injured body part or when the cause of the illness is known (like the flu); and red-orange, as energy for critical healing sent for severe illnesses and to help mend broken bones or wounds. There are many magical means to speed healing, from brews and potions to magic oils to special foods. Luckily, a large portion of the ingredients we need are readily available at the grocery store.

Brews

Healing…what a fabulous use for a witch's brew! As I said before, a bubbling cauldron filled with some magical elixir is personally extremely satisfying, not that you have to use a cauldron; you could use a regular kitchen pot. There are several recipes which are easily made and used to promote general good health, restore strength during illness, or even remove specific ailments. This first potion may be brewed and drunk regularly to maintain and strengthen general good health.

Good Health Potion

Honey is a magical substance, lemon is connected to the lunar energy and is purifying, ginger is good for digestion, and tea contains many healthful properties. All these combine to make a wonderful, vitalizing combination.

1 tablespoon honey

½ lemon

1 tiny pinch ginger

1 tea bag

2 cups water

Heat the water and brew the tea in your preferred manner. Next, pour some of the brewed tea into a cup and squeeze the juice of the lemon half through a small sieve (to avoid seeds) into the cup. Add the honey and a tiny pinch of ginger. Seriously, make sure it is tiny—just a whisper—since too much ginger can be overpowering. Stir to combine. Finally, holding your hands over the cup of tea, will your energy into the brew. Concentrate your desire for good health into the liquid, and drink it in for good health.

Healing Potion

The herbs in this recipe not only impart their nutritional and physical properties into this potion, which aids overall health, but their magical healing properties as well.

2 tablespoons rosemary

2 tablespoons spearmint

1 teaspoon sage

1 teaspoon thyme

½ lemon

1 tablespoon honey

2 cups water

Heat the water just below the boiling point (tiny bubbles appear at the bottom of the pot), then remove from heat. Add the herbs, cover, and let sit. Cool for ten to thirteen minutes, and then strain into a cup. Add the tablespoon of honey to the cup and squeeze in the juice of half a lemon over a sieve to catch seeds. Hold the cup of liquid in both hands, and send your energy into the potion along with your desire for healing. Slowly sip the potion, and visualize yourself in a strong, healthy state of being. Repeat daily as desired.

Stomach Tonic

This tonic helps to ease an upset stomach. The mint is added primarily to dull the flavor of the other herbs, but if you don't care for it, it may be used in lesser quantities or omitted entirely while keeping the tonic's overall effectiveness intact.

1 teaspoon dried marjoram

1 teaspoon dried thyme

1 teaspoon dried sage

1 tablespoon dried peppermint

2 cups water

Heat the water to just under boiling point. Add the herbs, cover, and remove from heat. Allow it to cool for at least ten minutes. Sweeten as desired, and sip slowly to bring relief.

Healing Bath Brew

> 1 tablespoon anise
>
> 3 bay leaves
>
> 1 garlic clove
>
> 1 tablespoon dried peppermint
>
> 1 tablespoon parsley
>
> 2 cups of water

Heat the water to just below the boiling point and add the herbs. Cover and remove from heat. Allow to cool for ten minutes, then strain. To use: run a bath and add a cup of sea salt (optional) to the water along with this brew. Step into the bath and soak for as long as desired while envisioning yourself in a healthy state.

Oils

Magical oils are not only excellent for dressing candles in ritual and magical work, but also a good means of receiving magical energy directly through the skin for issues such as muscle aches or healing of bruises or other injuries. That being said, do not apply magical oils to burned skin as the ingredients could be irritating.

Healing Oil

> 1 tablespoon rosemary
>
> 3 bay leaves, crumbled

1 tablespoon peppermint

½ cup olive oil

Mix the herbs in a bowl and empower them with your desire for healing. Pour the olive oil into a small pot and add the herbs into the oil, swirling them in. Over very low heat, warm the oil until you can smell the herbs in the air. When this occurs, remove from heat, cover, and allow it to cool for at least half an hour. When cooled, strain the oil into a bottle. Hold the bottle in both hands, and mentally (and emotionally) pour your energy and desire into the oil to charge it with healing power.

Extreme Healing Oil

This oil is called extreme for two reasons: it is a strong healing oil that should only be used when necessary, and its ingredients—namely tobacco—which, come on, you've got to admit *is* an interesting (if not ironic) idea. Tobacco has indeed been used for many magical purposes in the past, including healing, but nowadays I would not suggest any of the methods that involve smoking or ingesting the herb in any way. Using it in this form, however, is a safe alternative, provided you use only a pinch added *after* the oil has been bottled and you never use it as an anointing oil on the skin. Nobody needs nicotine soaking into their skin; that heals nothing. The oil is used, however, to anoint talismans and candles to speed healing of injuries and severe illness.

1 tablespoon sage

3 potato eyes

1 tablespoon rosemary

1 tablespoon thyme

1 pinch tobacco

1 cup olive oil

Charge the herbs and mix them in a small bowl (except the tobacco). Pour the oil into a small pot, add the herbs (again, except for the tobacco) and warm over low heat until you can smell the herbs in the air. Allow to cool, then strain and bottle. Add the pinch of tobacco to the bottle and charge the completed oil with visualised red-orange light and the intent of strong healing.

Remember that casting spells, even healing spells, on other people is unethical without their permission. No one should use magic to coerce another, even toward healing. Working against someone's free will is dangerous and opens us up to magical backlash, not to mention that doing so can interfere with the important lessons and future direction of someone's life. Always ask first before performing any magic on someone else. If that is impossible, a safe thing to do is send general energy to them as pure white light with the intent that if they subconsciously wish to accept it, it will go where it needs to be. Sending energy in this way can be a wonderful boost to somebody's own strength and can help in their healing and recovery. Assuming you have their permission or you are working for yourself, there are many magical possibilities for healing.

HEALING OIL SPELLS

Using oils in your magic gives you several options, such as personal anointing and candle magic as a means of casting a spell. This first spell is for the healing of *illness* (as opposed to *injuries*) and is designed to be used for people only. A separate spell will be given for the healing of animals.

Basic Candle Spell for Healing

Calm and center yourself. If desired, take a simple cleansing bath by pouring a cup of salt into a warm tub of water. After your bath, take a white candle and anoint it with Healing Oil while visualizing the person in need of healing in a perfectly healthy, strong, whole state. See this energy of pure, white light being poured *into* the candle and will it to be held there in the wax until it is released by the lighting of the candle. Once the candle is ready to be lit, set it on a low table and sit before the table. Strongly visualize a beam of white light coming from above, pouring into the body of the person to be healed. See the person as being filled with the universal white light and being fully healthy and strong. When you feel you have reached a peak, that the target of this spell is fully empowered by the light and healing energy, light the candle to send forth your spell while chanting the following:

Clear the block, imbalance purged.
Healing power, flow and surge!
Spirit power, beam of light,
Infuse the strength on one this night.
For good of all, for good of
She/he/me (depending),
As I do will, so shall it be!

Candle Spell for Speeding the Healing of Injuries

This spell is a bit more precise in that it targets a specific injury as opposed to sending energy toward healing of the whole body in general. Thus, before casting this spell, you need to have an understanding of what is injured and where on the person's body so you are sending the energy to the proper place. Once this is determined, you are ready to begin.

Obtain a red-orange candle, or if that cannot be found, one red candle and one orange candle. If using the two candle method, charge both candles with red-orange light. Red-orange is a color used to treat severe illness and injuries and is ideal to use in this type of magic.

When you are ready, first take a cleansing bath. Afterwards, set the candle(s) unlit on a low table. Incidentally, if you are using the two-candle method, place the red candle on the left side of the table and the orange candle on the right side. This keeps the energy flowing in the proper direction. If you are working for someone else, have a picture of them or a personal object such as hair, nail clippings, worn clothing, etc. on the table between the candles (if using two) or in front of the candle (if using one). Anoint the candle(s) and fill them with red-orange light. Settle yourself in front of the table and go into a meditative state. When you are ready, visualize the person with the injury, and see the injured part of the body surrounded by red-orange light and—this is *very* important—see the body part as completely whole, perfect and functional. Do not visualize it healing or becoming whole at all. Don't focus on the process, see only the result! When you feel the energy reach its peak, open your eyes and light the candle(s) to release the spell's energy. If you are using two candles, light the left one first, then the right one. As you light the candles, say the following spell:

> Surging strength, red-orange light;
> Rebuilt, empowered, healed, and mended.
> Flesh and bone filled with might,
> Strong and perfect; suffering ended.

Candle Spell for the Healing of Animals

Since they cannot talk, healing animals can be tricky. Under most circumstances, we can't have a regular dialogue with them to find out what the issue is. So, our main strategy should be to offer our animal friend energetic healing designed to heal whatever the trouble is.

First of all, if any animal (or person for that matter) has a serious illness or a broken limb, take them to the proper doctor. Magical healing is best used to speed recovery *after* the proper medical procedures have been employed. Our use of directed, empowered energy is an excellent tool to help the body ward off infection and strengthen the body's own healing abilities, but let's face it: you need to put a limb in a cast if that is what is required.

Here is a wonderfully simple spell to help empower an animal in distress so it can recover from an illness or injury. First, you will need the basic Healing Oil and a brown candle. You will also need a picture of the animal and/or a lock of its fur or feathers, depending. If the animal in question is in a cage or aquarium, cast the spell in the same room as the animal. It is recommended that you do not cast the spell near the animal if it is not confined, as it may knock over the candle and start a fire.

To begin the spell, take a cleansing bath in blessed, salted water. After your bath, go to your working area, anoint the brown candle with the Healing Oil, and hold it. Gaze at the animal if present, the photo, or the lock of fur/feather, etc. Visualize the animal in a perfectly healthy, strong state of being. In your mind's eye, see it surrounded by a bright brown light with white edges; see the animal glowing with this energy, being perfectly happy. During the visualization, infuse a feeling of joy and relief (if that is how you want to feel when your healing goal is reached) into the image. When you feel ready, open your eyes, set the candle on the table, and light it as you chant the spell:

> *Fin and feather; flesh, fur, and bone;*
> *My animal friend with healing imbued;*

Healthy and well, strong and whole,
Encircled in light; restored and renewed!

Powders

Healing powder can be used for a few different tasks: making a simple version of herb candles, pouring in a ring around a spell candle, or sprinkling as a powder to generate an aura of healing energy. Powders are easy to make and are good to have around as simple, convenient magical items to use on a moment's notice.

Healing Powder

> 1 tablespoon sage
>
> 2 teaspoons marjoram or oregano
>
> 2 teaspoons spearmint
>
> 1 tablespoon cornstarch

Charge each herb with the quality of healing and grind each separately before combining them all with the cornstarch. Once the cornstarch has been added, bottle the completed powder and dedicate it to the purpose of healing.

Healing Powder Spells

The first spell you could use is a candle spell using herb candles. To make a simple herb candle, all you have to do is take a white candle, a light blue candle, or a red-orange candle (for critical healing), lightly anoint it with either Healing Oil or pure olive oil, and then roll the candle in the Healing Powder to create a perfectly coated herb candle. One word of caution: only anoint and coat the sides of the candle, not the bottom or the top by the wick. When the candle burns, you don't want the powder to catch fire; you just need the energy from the powder to absorb into and combine with the power of the candle. The powder itself doesn't need to burn. The herb candle can be used in the following spell.

Herb Candle of Healing Light

Create the herb candle (wax of the proper color; white, light blue, or red-orange, depending on the ailment) and charge it with your desire for healing (whether for yourself or another) by seeing a clear mental image of yourself (or the chosen recipient) in perfect health. When this image is built up strongly in your mind, send the energy down to your dominant hand and into the candle, charging it with power. When you wish to cast the spell, set the candle on your spell table and again focus on the desired goal by visualizing a perfectly healed state. When you are ready, light the candle and chant the following spell:

> *Current of power, shining light;*
> *Healing energy, burning bright;*
> *Healed and strong, imbalance ceased;*
> *React and respond, purge and release.*

Once the spell has been cast, allow the candle to burn itself out if it is safe to do so or just let it burn for as long as possible before extinguishing. If desired, you may recast this spell over several consecutive nights until the candle is completely used.

You can modify the above spell: instead of making an herb candle with the powder, charge the candle as is and then pour a ring of the Healing Powder around the candle to lend its energy to your spell. This is ideal when you are out of the proper oil and don't have the time or ingredients to make more right away. It is best if you set the candle and circle of powder on a large plate or pentacle platter so as not to ruin the table with the powder. After this is done, continue with the above spell as described.

Circle of Magic

For this spell, you will need a considerable amount of Healing Powder, at least quadruple the recipe. The structure of this spell is to create a circle of Healing Powder large enough to sit in and absorb the healing energy. This is best done outdoors for two reasons: first, to minimize any damage caused by pouring powder around (no ruining carpeting this way) and second, to draw upon the healing power of the earth herself. First, once you have made the appropriate amount of Healing Powder, go to an outdoor location where you can sit for a while (at least fifteen minutes) and work the magic. Choose a day that is not too windy, or you could end up with a billowing cloud of powder in the air. When you arrive at your location, pour the Healing Powder *carefully* onto the ground in a circle roughly three or four feet in diameter in which to sit.

Once you have the completed circle on the ground, step in and sit down. Close your eyes and relax. Do the Autumn Tree Meditation (see chapter 2) and when you reach the inner door, step through and see either a bluish-white or (for critical healing of severe problems only) a red-orange circle of light glowing on the ground. In your mind's eye, see yourself seated within this glowing circle. Watch the circle's light flowing up to you and being absorbed into your body. Float with this energy for a time (fifteen minutes to half an hour is ideal). When you are ready, visualize the circle of light sinking into the earth to ground and dissipate. Then bring yourself out of the meditation.

How this particular magic works is that you are physically within a healing circle of charged Healing Powder. Mentally and spiritually, you are placing yourself within an energetic healing circle of light (the astral equivalent of the circle of powder) to fully absorb healing energy at all three levels of the psyche: mental, spiritual, and physical. As a result, you gain magical aid to help heal the body at all levels. If you wish to tailor the energy to a specific goal, instead of absorbing it into your whole body, visualize it being absorbed into the location of the actual trouble and concentrate it there.

Charms

There are a couple of charms that can be easily made from supermarket items. First, you can make a healing herb bath sachet. Using a coffee filter, add equal parts dried rosemary, thyme, basil, and sage and secure the little bundle with a twist tie. Charge the sachet with healing energy and store in a jar in a cool, dry place. To use, simply place the sachet in the bathtub before running the water. As you fill the tub with warm water, the essence will be steeped out of the herbs, making the bath basically a giant brew. By bathing in it, you transfer the healing essence from the herbs into your body.

Nutty Healing Charm

Another good healing charm can be made from a walnut. Nuts, being seeds, are loaded with the generative energy of creation. This energy is concerned with growth and the building of cells and physical strength. This is the ideal type of energy to be used in healing or fertility magic. All you have to do to activate this energy is charge it with your intent of health, healing, or fertility and carry it with you wherever you go so that you will absorb its essence. If you wish to conceal it in a charm bag, use the colors green or white. This won't diminish its strength in any way. Walnuts are good ingredients (whether in food or magic) to use when wishing to heal the mind or brain. It has been said that walnuts help to cure madness. While this has not been an issue for me, thankfully, I do know that walnuts contain omega-3 fatty acids which indeed are good for the brain. Maybe walnuts really do help with such ills.

Foods

Ah, food. Where would we be without good, real food? My definition of real food is a little different from that of most people: for me, food has to be nutritious and as close to whole as possible in order to qualify. Cake is not real food. Since this chapter is on healing, we need to discuss some fundamental truths about food. We need food—good food, real food, and a lot of it—in order to be healthy. This of course is not a diet and exercise book, but since we are talking about healing, I feel impelled to state three *very* important things.

1. If you gain nothing else from this book, know—*truly know*—that you need calories and nutrients to live and thrive. Never cut calories, even to lose weight. This is a dangerous practice that throws the body into starvation mode and leads to loss of muscle tissue and the actual *storage* of body fat. Unless you are totally sedentary, you should take your current body weight and add a zero; that number is roughly how many calories you should consume **daily** to stay metabolically active.

2. There are three sources of food energy: carbohydrates at 4 calories per gram, proteins at 4 calories per gram, and fats at 9 calories per gram; fats have more than twice as many calories as the other two sources of energy.

3. If you wish to lose weight, increase aerobic
   activity to a minimum of 30 minutes four
   times a week and cut the amount of fat in
   your diet to between 10 and 30 percent.
   Do not lower your caloric intake! Don't do it!
   NEVER! Fat must be burned off, not starved
   off. If you starve yourself, you lose water first
   and then lean muscle. If your body is deprived,
   it holds on to fat as long as it can in order to
   survive. Diets don't work—cutting out dietary
   fat and burning off your stored fat works.

Okay, rant over. The reason I state this is that any practitioner must be relatively healthy in order to be successful with magic. If you are starving all the time; you place yourself in a weakened, non-magical state. It is very difficult to manifest your desires on the material plane when you are weakened and malnourished.

If you eat whole, real food, you are more likely to maintain overall good health than if you eat the mostly processed, chemically preserved kind. Our bodies are designed to metabolize and use food as fuel to power all the functions and processes that keep us alive. The healthier the fuel, the healthier the person, generally. Our bodies have no need for chemical preservatives, processed and bleached starches, or overly fatty food products. Since we have no need for these things, your body must cleanse itself of what become impurities in the system.

All whole, real, natural foods have healing ability. Things that we transform *into* food do not. Apples and carrots help the body to restore itself whereas candy and cheeseburgers don't. Things like that make the body work even harder to maintain its balance and rid itself of toxins. Whole foods are foods eaten in their complete state (or as complete as possible) such as peaches or baked potatoes in their skins. Keep in mind that whole doesn't mean raw. Whole foods can be cooked and eaten to bring their healing properties within.

My recommendations for healing foods are onions and garlic as often as possible, and fruits, vegetables, beans, and grains as you can fit into your diet. Culinary herbs and spices are also good items to add to food as often as you can. Cinnamon, for example, helps lower blood sugar. If you have a problem with high blood sugar, you may want to add a little cinnamon to your shopping list. Also, fresh herbs like basil or marjoram can be added to salads and sandwiches for their flavor and added nutrients.

If you are ill, cut out heavy, oily, sugary, and/or starchy foods, since these take energy away from your body while providing little to no nutritional value. Soup, of course, is a wonderful healing food since it is warm, soothing, and keeps the body hydrated and nourished while not being overly filling. People can usually tolerate at least a little soup, even if they are having trouble eating during their illness. The following recipe is my own creation and is filled with many healing ingredients. It's my take on a classic healing food: chicken soup.

Chicken Soup à la Furie

- 2 pieces boneless, skinless, chicken breast (half breast), cubed

- 1 medium onion, chopped

- 1 stalk celery, cut lengthwise, then chopped

- 2 carrots, chopped

- 1 tomato, chopped

- 1 clove garlic, minced

- 5 cups water

- 1 ½ cups egg noodles

- 2 chicken bouillon cubes

- 1 teaspoon salt

- ¼ cup parsley

- 1 bay leaf

Cook the cubed chicken pieces lightly (about two to three minutes on each side, turning once) in a frying pan with the garlic, and drain away any excess grease. Next, add the water and bouillon cubes to a stock pot along with all the other ingredients except for the chicken. Cook for about ten to fifteen minutes until vegetables and noodles are tender. Add the chicken and cook for five more minutes. Remove from heat. As the soup cools, hold your hands over it high enough so as not to give yourself a steam burn, and visualize healing energy (blue and/or white light) coming from your hands and third eye pouring into the soup. Declare to yourself that the soup is a healing food according to free will and for the good of all. The soup is now ready to serve. Note: if you are a vegetarian (as I am), you could swap out vegetable broth for the bouillon and 3 cups of cubed potatoes for the chicken.

Healing and Fertility

Restoring fertility is a wonderful and truly magical act. So many people have fertility issues but don't have the thousands of dollars needed to pay for special medical treatments. A wonderful and much less expensive route to try first is using magic to revive the body's fertility. Since fertility magic is an act of restoring balance to the body, I have grouped it in this chapter. If your healing goal centers on fertility, you can add a hazelnut (also called a filbert) and some poppy seeds to the healing walnut charm mentioned earlier. Place all these into the charm bag and charge it with your desire for fertility: hold the bag in both hands and breathe your desire into it before tying it shut.

As previously stated, *Supermarket Magic* is not intended to be a cookbook, but when healing and fertility are concerned, food is of utmost importance. Here are two wonderful recipes that combine several fertility restoring ingredients: figs, eggs, coconut, and hazelnuts.

Olive and Fig Tapenade (dip)

1 cup chopped dried figs

½ cup water

1 tablespoon olive oil

2 tablespoons balsamic vinegar

1 teaspoon dried rosemary

1 teaspoon dried thyme

¼ teaspoon cayenne pepper

⅔ cup chopped kalamata olives

2 cloves garlic, minced

salt and pepper to taste

⅓ cup chopped toasted walnuts

1 (8 ounce) package cream cheese

Put the figs and water into a pot and bring them to a boil until the figs are tender and liquid has reduced. Use low heat and let them cook for 10 minutes or so. For me at least, it is a good idea to use kitchen scissors to cut up the dried rosemary in little pieces and add it to the boiling figs so they soften in the water as well. Remove from heat and stir in the olive oil, balsamic vinegar, herbs, salt, black pepper, and cayenne pepper. Add olives and garlic and mix well. Cover and refrigerate for a few hours to overnight. Before serving, place both hands over the bowl of tapenade and charge it with your desire for fertility. Visualize a warm glow in the area of the body needing to be restored (depending on gender) and feel the joy and relief of healing. When you are ready, mentally transfer this energy into the tapenade. Next, unwrap the cream cheese and place on a serving plate. Spoon the olive mixture over the cheese and sprinkle walnuts on top. Serve with slices of toasted french bread, crackers, or vegetable sticks.

No-Bake Fig and Hazelnut Balls

1 (8 ounce) package cream cheese, softened

½ cup butter, softened

¼ cup sifted powdered sugar

1 tablespoon milk (if needed, for smooth consistency)

⅓ cup finely chopped dried figs

⅓ cup toasted hazelnuts, chopped

¾ cup shredded coconut, sweetened is best

Mash together the cream cheese, butter, powdered sugar, and milk (if needed) to make a thick, frosting-like paste. Beat with electric hand mixer on medium speed, about a minute or until combined and a bit fluffy, like meringue. Stir in figs and hazelnuts. Chill the mixture for 30 minutes to an hour or until it's firm and easy to handle (a bit like making chocolate truffles). Using your hands, a small ice cream scoop, or a melon baller, depending on the size you want, shape mixture into balls. Roll the balls in the coconut flakes. Once all the balls are made, charge them with your desire for fertility as in the previous recipe. Serve immediately or cover in plastic wrap and store in the refrigerator until serving time.

Magic Snack

For a healthy snack that also improves fertility, combine sunflower seeds, chopped hazelnuts, raisins, and chopped dates with some sweetened coconut flakes to create a kind of magical trail mix. Charge the mix with your magical goal and eat as desired.

Bath Salts

Bath salts are an excellent means of relieving sore muscles and a way to absorb magical energy that has been placed into the salts. Soaking in a tub of warm water softens the skin, and the bath salts help to make it more receptive to cleansing and absorption. The following recipes are combined to make a bath salt to relieve stiff muscles and aches and pains.

Peppermint Oil

3 tablespoons peppermint (fresh or dried)

½ cup vegetable oil (soybean)

Optional: 3 drops of peppermint extract
(added after the oil is complete)

In a small pot, swirl the peppermint into the oil, and warm the mixture over very low heat until you can smell the herb in the air. At this point, remove from heat and allow to cool. When cooled, strain and bottle the oil. If desired, add the peppermint extract.

Peppermint Bath Salts

3 cups of Epsom salts

2 cups sea salt

1 cup baking soda

1 tablespoon (½ ounce) peppermint oil

Mix all ingredients together and empower with your desire for healing and relaxation.

To use, add from ¼ cup to 2 cups of bath salts per bath. If you have dry skin, use ¼ cup at first and experiment with lager amounts as desired. Soak for 20 minutes in the bath, and feel the muscle ache and stiffness improve.

Shopping List

Here's a short list of the ingredients used in the spells and recipes in this chapter.

❏ Almond	❏ Cream cheese	❏ Peppermint
❏ Anise	❏ Dates	❏ Poppy seeds
❏ Apple	❏ Egg noodles	❏ Potatoes

❏ Balsamic vinegar	❏ Epsom salts	❏ Powdered sugar
❏ Basil	❏ Figs	❏ Raisins
❏ Bay leaves	❏ Garlic	❏ Rosemary
❏ Black pepper	❏ Ginger	❏ Sage
❏ Butter	❏ Green juices	❏ Salt (sea salt or regular)
❏ Baking soda	❏ Hazel nuts	❏ Spearmint
❏ Candles (white, red-orange, brown, light blue)	❏ Honey	❏ Sunflower seeds
❏ Carrots	❏ Kalamata olives	❏ Tea
❏ Cayenne pepper	❏ Lemon	❏ Thyme
❏ Celery	❏ Lettuce	❏ Tobacco
❏ Chicken breast	❏ Marjoram/ oregano	❏ Tomato
❏ Cloves	❏ Milk	❏ Vegetable bouillon cubes
❏ Coconut	❏ Olive oil	❏ Vegetable oil
❏ Coffee filters	❏ Onions	❏ Walnuts
❏ Cornstarch	❏ Parsley	❏ Water

CHAPTER 7
Love, Lust, and Beauty Magic

When heading to the market to buy groceries, we're not usually thinking about love magic…I know that love and broccoli have never mixed well in my mind! But did you know that there are tons of options at the store for casting a spell of love? Of course, we must be very cautious when using magic to find love. This type of working, above all others, *must* be done with the "for the good of all" intention added to it. You really, really should never cast a love spell to gain the love of a specific person. While it is understood that this is unethical magic, that reason is all too often an insufficient deterrent. The call of "the one," that strongly yearned-for lover seen only through the idealized haze of their admirer, is frequently so powerful that all common sense is overwhelmed, and we give in to the temptation to misuse our magic and cast a manipulative spell.

If we cast a spell to gain the love of a specific person and we are successful, we are then extremely vulnerable to suffering several different consequences. The first potential consequence we might encounter is that once our idealized haze is pierced by the reality of having "the one" sitting in our living room hogging the remote and burping the alphabet, we may decide that we don't really like them so much anymore and want to be rid of them… only to find that they are deeply devoted to us and would *never* leave us, no matter how much we want to end things.

Another consequence of casting a love spell for a specific person's affection is that if we are casting a spell for him or her with specific qualities that we think we enjoy, it may also attract a great many others who share those same qualities. Yay! Lots of hangers-on who will all be fixated on you! The misery of unwelcome attention.

Perhaps the most difficult consequence is that when a person is "magically captured," they are essentially bound against their free will. While they do not consciously realize this, they know it subconsciously and will strike out accordingly. It is only natural to resent being bound and enslaved to another's will. When someone is under magical influence, they are *always* subconsciously aware of it. Their mind may not be powerful enough to break the spell, but a defense mechanism will kick in, resisting it. This resistance will show itself in continual arguments and episodes of conflict in the "relationship" which will ultimately sour it and create a need for separation.

Don't I make it all sound wonderful? Well I'm sorry, but it is every witch's responsibility to warn against the misuse of magic in an authentic manner. It's better to explain why not to misuse your skills, instead of just giving a blanket "don't do it," which explains nothing.

Now for the good news: you can use magic to gain love as often as you wish, but not for a specific person. If there are certain qualities you require a potential love to possess, it is fine to include those as conditions of your spell; just use care. In a love spell, more than any other type, it is imperative that you focus on how you wish to *feel* when your goal is achieved. If you focus on how you want to feel, the feeling becomes the top priority in the magic. The emphasis on feeling overrides anything in the spell that would counteract bringing it to you. If you combine proper feeling with "according to free will and only for good," you have created your ticket out of magical mistakes (in most cases). As long as you avoid manipulation or dominance, everything should work out fine.

Okay, enough nagging and warning and guiding and tutoring (and more nagging); time for the spells. Love spells are fun, fabulous, magnetic, sexy, and luckily really easy to make straight out of the grocery store! Let's start with my favorite magical concoctions, brews.

Brews

Ah, brews. Stirring the cauldron, cackling, tossing in herbs, cackling, watching the steam rise, cackling, charging the mystical infusion, cackling, and, of course, cackling. Okay, *maybe* not so much cackling. Anyway, there are many liquids that have been associated with love, libido, and sex. Wine is one, as is mulled apple cider. This section is not so focused on the idea of love potions as much as brews that can be used in conjunction with other spells. Administering a love potion to someone in hopes of gaining their love is, as we discussed, unethical magic.

The first recipe is a non-alcoholic cider drink that you can use as a libation or offering in spells designed to bring love into your life. You can also drink it to infuse yourself with loving vibrations and an aura of attractiveness.

Cider of Love

1 orange

15 cloves

4 cinnamon sticks

15 allspice berries

1 teaspoon of nutmeg

7 cardamom pods

¼ cup brown sugar

½ gallon of fresh, unfiltered apple cider

Pour apple cider into a 3-quart pot, cover, turn the heat on medium. While cider is warming, quarter the orange (with the peel intact; stem removed) and add the slices to the pot, along with the spices and brown sugar. Keep covered and heat the mulled cider mixture to a simmer and reduce heat to low. Simmer for 20 minutes on low heat.

After 20 minutes, remove from heat and strain cider away from the orange bits and spices. Charge the mixture with the energy of love. Serve hot or chilled. You can store the cider in the refrigerator in a pitcher, and this recipe makes 8 cups. To increase your chances, drink a cup of it each night for a week during the waxing moon while looking for love.

Magical Love Wine

1 bottle of red wine (your choice)

1 teaspoon cinnamon

½ teaspoon nutmeg

¼ teaspoon ginger

1 teaspoon vanilla extract

Mix and empower the spices and add them to the wine. Add the vanilla extract and re-cork the bottle. Let the wine sit for at least three days in a cool, dark place before serving. This wine can be served to one you love to increase the loving feelings between the two of you, served with someone's knowledge and consent, of course. This wine makes a good compliment to a romantic dinner, but can also be used by one person alone—drink it to enhance your attractive nature. If you intend to use it by yourself, it is probably best to cut the recipe in half or take as one small glass a day for a week or until the wine is gone.

Tea of Desire

This potion increases lust and passion and can be consumed by couples to increase their desire.

1 black tea bag (regular tea)

½ teaspoon lemon juice

½ teaspoon orange juice

1 pinch coriander

½ teaspoon dried mint

¼ teaspoon nutmeg

3 cups water

Heat the water to just under the boiling point (bubbles appearing at the bottom of the pot), add all the ingredients, and remove from heat. Allow to cool for a few minutes and charge with your intent. Strain, sweeten if desired, and serve.

Coffee Aphrodisiac

If you prefer coffee to tea, you may want to try this recipe. Some people have sensitive stomachs, and they may be bothered by coffee's acidity. If you are not a regular coffee drinker, now would not be the time to start. There is nothing more unsexy than an upset stomach. For those who enjoy coffee, this recipe is rather simple to prepare.

2-4 tablespoons ground regular
(or decaffeinated, if you prefer) coffee

¼ teaspoon cardamom

6 cups water

Honey (to sweeten)

Creamer (optional)

Mix the coffee grounds and cardamom together in a small dish and charge them with your aphrodisiac intent. Next, place the mixture in the filter of your coffee maker and fill it with 6 cups of water or your preferred amount. Turn on the coffee maker. Once the coffee has brewed, pour into two mugs and sweeten to taste with the honey, adding creamer as desired. Sip the coffee slowly and relax.

Chamomile Attraction Bath Brew

6 chamomile tea bags

3 cups of water

Brew the chamomile tea and add it to your bath water. Bathing in chamomile increases your attraction and draws potential lovers to you.

Love Perfume

1 teaspoon mixed spice (see below)

½ cup ethyl alcohol

To make a love perfume, you will need a bottle of ethyl rubbing alcohol (not isopropyl), which can usually be found in the health and beauty aisle of most large supermarkets or chain pharmacies. You will also need some cinnamon, nutmeg, allspice, ginger, and powdered cloves. To save money and time, just grab one of those little bottles of pumpkin pie spice, which is a combination of those spices. In a jar, mix a teaspoon of spice to a half cup of alcohol. Seal the jar and keep in a cool dry place for two weeks, shaking the bottle daily to mix the spices. After two weeks, strain the liquid through a coffee filter to get the spices out and rebottle the brownish liquid. Charge the liquid to be a perfume of attraction. Afterwards, you can place a dab on each of your pulse points and an aura of attraction will surround you.

Oils

As previously noted, magical oils are a very versatile product. You can use magical love-drawing oils as perfume, to anoint charms, or to anoint candles or papers used in spellwork. The following oil is a simple love oil, easily made for use in all your love magic.

Love Oil

½ cup olive oil

1 tablespoon apple peel

1 teaspoon coriander seed

1 teaspoon strawberry stems (or leaves)

Simmer the peel, coriander, and strawberry leaves in the oil until their scent is transferred, then let the oil cool. Strain the oil and charge it with the intent to draw love. Bottle for use.

Oil Spells

Aside from using a love-drawing oil as a perfume to anoint the body to give yourself a magical aura of attraction, there are other uses for the oil, like candle magic.

Bond of Love

Note: This spell should only be done by heterosexuals unless properly modified (see below). It is designed to work with that polarized energy. To cast this spell, you will need the following items.

1 jar of ground cinnamon
(1 to 2 ounce spice bottles)

1 jar of ground nutmeg
(1 to 2 ounce spice bottles)

Small glass cruet (or funnel) and bowl

2 candles (1 pink and 1 blue)

Disposable white or pink tablecloth or towel
(not plastic or vinyl; biodegradable fabric!)

Love Oil

Before casting this spell, take a cleansing bath and focus only on the feeling of the love you want to bring into your life. When you are finished bathing, go to your altar table, lay out the tablecloth, and charge the bottles of spices: the nutmeg with the power of feminine sexuality and love and the cinnamon with the power of masculine sexuality and love. Now pour and mix the spices together in the bowl or cruet. If using the funnel, slowly pour the mix of spices through the funnel; if using the cruet, simply pour the spices from it. Either way, slowly pour the spices into a lemniscate (sideways figure 8) shape on the cloth.

Make the figure 8 shape large enough to fit the candles inside the loops of the 8. Next, on the blue candle carve the male symbol ($\male$) and on the pink candle carve the female symbol ($\female$). Hold the female candle in the left hand and the male candle in the right hand and squeeze them until you can feel your hands pulsing. Mentally pour the energy and desire to bring love into your life into the candles while you hold them. When you feel ready, anoint each candle with love oil and set the female candle in the left loop of the figure 8 and the male candle in the right loop.

Close your eyes and focus ONLY on the feeling you want to have when in a perfect, happy relationship. Feel your desire fully and immerse yourself in this energy. Imagine yourself spending time with your ideal mate (remember, no specific people; keep it general) and when you are energized and strong in your power, light the candles, first left then right, and chant the following spell as you pour out the desire and energy toward your goal (imagine spending time with your ideal mate and send the power to this image):

> *Spirit cord, seal the bond.*
> *Perfect balance, figure eight;*
> *Magic power bring to me*
> *My heart's great joy; true love's mate.*

If possible and safe to do so, allow the candles to burn out completely on their own. If not, let them burn for as long as possible before extinguishing them, starting with the left one using a candle snuffer or the back of a spoon. When the candles have completely cooled, gather up the corners of the cloth with the candles and spices contained inside and bury them in the ground with thanks.

To modify: Use only a single color for the candles (pink, blue, or lavender, if you prefer) and use nutmeg (for lesbians) or cinnamon (for gay men) only, without the other spice, in which case you will need two jars of the chosen single spice. The chant can remain as is and all other steps remain the same.

Charms

Love charms are a classic magical item. Luckily, there are loads of options at the store for creating charms so we don't have to go hunting for bird feathers, shells, crystals, or rare herbs, or forge our own sigil on metal medallions (not a skill of mine). In the past, gathering exotic magical ingredients was a sign of your sincerity and determination to reach your goal. While this does have validity, these days, even though we may be quite determined and very sincere, we are often too busy to go on a drawn-out quest for ingredients and then do a complex ritual with what we've gathered.

I know that I, for one, almost never have a full day with nothing else to do other than the magic or ritual I have planned. There are always so many other mundane obligations to wade through first. That's why I always include a shopping list at the end of each chapter; all we need to do is add those items to our normal grocery lists and get everything bought all at once. It's also usually far less expensively than if we bought items at specialty stores individually. Consider your convenience and cost issues (mostly) solved.

Now, on to love charms. There are a few different options; the first is an herbal charm bag.

Charm Bag
Love Charm

    1 chamomile tea bag

    1 pinch basil

1 pinch cinnamon

1 pinch oregano or marjoram

If you wish to make a charm bag to attract love, then we have two stops to make. First, go to the aisle that has dried herbs and grab bottles of basil, cinnamon, and oregano. Next, go and get a box of chamomile tea. When you get home, open the chamomile tea bag carefully and pour the chamomile into a bowl. Add a pinch of basil, cinnamon, and oregano to the bowl. Mix everything around with your fingers. Charge the herbs to bring you love. Now place the mixed herbs back in the tea bag and either re-staple or tie it closed with pink cord or ribbon. Carry the bag with you wherever you go.

PENNIES OF LOVE

2 pennies

1 red candle

1 pink candle

Love Oil (see page 125 in this chapter)

Heat-proof plate

This charm is designed to bring an ideal mate to you. For the pennies, you have two options; the first one is to use shiny new pennies from the current year and the second option is to use pennies minted in the year you were born.

Either way, doing so will boost your luck in finding love. The basic mechanics of this charm consist of blessing the pennies and joining them together with the wax from both candles. Three days before you begin this spell, soak the pennies in blessed saltwater to remove any previous energies they may contain. On the day you wish to create this charm, gather together all the items needed and place them on your altar table. Wash off the pennies to remove the saltwater and dry them completely. Charge the candles with your desire for love. Set the red candle on the left side of the plate and the pink one on the right side. Go into a meditation while holding the pennies, and visualize the type of person you wish to meet. When you have a clear mental image built up, make sure to focus on how you want to feel in the relationship. Mentally transfer this feeling into the pennies, visualizing pink light flowing through your arms and into the pennies.

When you feel ready, set the pennies on the plate and light the candles, starting with the red one. As they flame up, focus on a warm, contented feeling of happiness. Continue to think about the type of person you want to attract. When the candles have burned and some wax has melted, carefully pick up the red candle and drip a little wax onto one penny. Set the red candle down and pick up the pink candle. Drip some pink wax on the other penny. Set the pink candle down and before the wax hardens completely, pick up the pennies and press them together, wax sides in. Set the pennies back on the plate and pick up the red candle and drip red wax all over the top of the joined pennies. When it is completely covered, set the red candle down and turn the pennies over. Pick up the pink candle and drip wax all over the other side of the pennies until it is completely covered as well. When finished, you should no longer be able to see the pennies, just wax with one side red and the other side pink.

Finally, hold the penny charm in both hands and send pink light into it one more time while strongly visualizing being in a happy relationship. When you feel empowered, chant this spell to bind your intent into the charm:

Magic of Venus, copper coins,
Bring to me an ideal mate.
Real love, hearts enjoined,
Hurry forth; end this wait.
Charm of love, my desire impart,
Currents of love draw her/him to my heart.

Carry the penny charm with you in a red or pink charm bag if possible, and/or sleep with it under your pillow at night.

Bath Salts

To infuse yourself with loving vibrations, you can make bath salts charged with loving energy. To do this is a bit complicated though. First, you need Epsom salts (check the health and beauty aisle), some regular salt, and baking soda. You also need red food coloring and a small bottle of Love Oil.

Love Bath Salts

    3 cups Epsom salts

    2 cups sea salt

    1 cup baking soda

    1 tablespoon (½ ounce) Love Oil

    A few drops red food coloring

Mix the Epsom salt, sea salt, and baking soda together. Now, add the oil a few drops at a time, being careful not to add too much. The consistency should be fairly dry, like damp sand, not oily salt-soup. Once you have added enough oil, put a few drops of red food color in and mix. The bath salt should come out looking pink. Once made, the bath salt should be charged to bring loving energies to anyone who uses it. To use, add ¼ cup to ½ cup to a warm bath and relax in the water, soaking in the loving energy.

Beauty

Beauty-Enhancing Scrub

    3 tablespoons granulated sugar

    1 tablespoon olive oil

Pour the sugar into a small container, and add the olive oil. Stir with the forefinger (pointing finger) of your strong hand, and empower the mixture with your desire for enhanced beauty.

To use: Apply the mixture to the facial area slowly (and gently) in circular motions to exfoliate and moisturize the skin. After you have finished scrubbing your face, rinse the sugar mixture off in tepid water and wash your face with your usual facial soap.

Glamour Spell for Makeup

Chosen makeup

1 pink candle

Love Oil (see page 125)

You can magically enhance your normal, everyday makeup and skincare products to create a powerful energy of attraction and beauty around yourself every time you wear them. To do so, take the chosen makeup to your altar-table. Anoint a pink candle with Love Oil and light it. Settle yourself before the altar and go into a meditation while holding the makeup. When you are relaxed, imagine a powerful magnetic, glimmering energy pouring through you, into your hands, and from them into the makeup. Visualize this energy building in the bottle until you feel the bottle pulsing with magnetic energy. When you feel the makeup is full of the energy, chant the following to program the energy and activate the glamour:

Faery magic, velvet haze;
Wrap me in your shimmering light.
Glittering aura, beauty amaze,

Blemishes blurred; glamour takes flight.
For good of all, by my true will,
Makeup charged; promise fulfill!

Whenever you use this makeup, it will help create extra beauty and attractiveness around you. This effect will last for as long as you are wearing that application of makeup. When you wash it off, the glamour fades, and when you reapply, the glamour is restored. You can use this spell on all your makeup and skin care products, if desired.

Foods

There is of course a lot of food at a supermarket, and some of it can be used to draw love to you. Keep in mind, however, that it is a bad idea to try to manipulate a specific person into loving you. Using food in love magic is best left to creating or keeping loving harmony between existing loved ones as opposed to drawing in new loved ones. Some of the more popular foods of love are oysters (barring allergies, of course) chocolate, strawberries, vanilla, and red wine. Any food made to have a magical effect must be charged to do so, otherwise its effect will be minimal.

Aphrodisiac Recipes

These foods when prepared alone or in combination increase attraction, sexuality, and the bonds of love when consumed by a couple. Since I am a Leo and most of us are dessert-first kind of people, I will start with recipes for a banana split and a magical chocolate cake.

Banana Split (of Love)

> 3 scoops of ice cream (vanilla, or 1 scoop
>   each chocolate, strawberry, and vanilla)
>
> 1 banana
>
> 100% fruit strawberry jam
>
> 100% fruit apricot jam
>
> Chocolate sauce

Cut the banana lengthwise and place in a dish. Place the three scoops of ice cream in between the banana halves and spoon one topping on each scoop according to taste. If the jams are too thick, you can warm them in a sauce pan to create a more syrupy texture. Hold your hands over the completed banana split and charge it with your desire to increase love. Then, it's time to eat!

Each of the chosen sauces as well as each of the possible ice creams are naturally filled with energies attuned to love magic. The banana, though tuned more toward abundance, has a shape that could be said to evoke thoughts of passion. And abundance in love is a good thing, anyway.

Chocolate Cake (of Love)

2 cups flour

1 ¾ cups sugar

¾ cup baking cocoa

1 ¼ cups milk

¾ cup butter (not margarine), softened

3 eggs

1 teaspoon baking soda

1 teaspoon salt

1 teaspoon vanilla extract

½ teaspoon baking powder

Preheat the oven to 350 degrees. Measure all dry ingredients into a mixing bowl. Make a well in the center, and add the eggs. Mix gently with a fork to bring a bit of the dry ingredients into the eggs. Now add the milk and mix lightly again just to combine a bit more. Add the softened butter, and use an electric hand mixer (if desired) to mix the rest of the way. Continue beating on low until thoroughly mixed, then increase speed to medium for two minutes. Grease and flour two 9-inch round cake pans. Pour half of the cake batter into each pan. Trace either a pentagram or heart shape into the batter while charging with your intent and bake for 30 to 35 minutes. Cool cakes in their pans on wire racks for 10 minutes, then remove cakes from pans. Allow each cake to cool completely before frosting.

Frosting

    2 cups confectioner's (powdered) sugar

    ½ cup butter, softened

    3 tablespoons milk

    1 ½ teaspoons vanilla extract

    ⅛ teaspoon salt

    3 squares baking chocolate

    2 egg yolks

Add first five ingredients in a mixing bowl. In a double boiler, melt the chocolate squares. Once they are completely melted, stir in the egg yolks. Remove from heat and combine in the mixing bowl with the other ingredients. With large fork or hand mixer at medium speed, beat until smooth. If the consistency is too thick, you can add one more tablespoon of milk. Smooth out the surface then trace a pentagram or heart shape in the frosting while charging with your intent before using.

The active magical ingredients in both the cake and frosting are flour, since wheat is related to fertility; milk and eggs, which are also related to fertility; sugar, since it is dedicated to Venus, the goddess and planet of love; chocolate, a powerful aphrodisiac; butter, a symbol of transformation tied to the faery realm; and finally, vanilla, a classic ingredient for both love and lust. As you can see, this recipe combines several strong ingredients, and when charged with magic to focus their intent, a simple chocolate cake becomes an amazing love and passion-enhancing food.

Pesto (of Love)

⅓ cup olive oil

¼ cup grated parmesan cheese

¼ cup parsley

1 garlic clove, minced

½ cup fresh basil leaves, chopped
   (or 2 tablespoons dried basil)

1 teaspoon salt

¼ teaspoon ground nutmeg

Mix all ingredients in a blender on medium until well combined. Pour the pesto into a bowl. Hold your hands over the bowl and charge with your desire for peace, love, and happiness. Olive oil promotes peace, basil and nutmeg promote love, and the garlic, salt, and parsley promote purification and healing. This mixture is very good to add to pasta or chicken dishes when trying to promote love and goodwill, and also when trying to reconcile after an argument.

Tomato and Leek Soup (of Love)

Tomato, basil, and leek soup is a classic Italian dish. Luckily for us, these ingredients—specifically the basil, leeks, tomatoes, and carrots—are perfect for inspiring feelings of love and romance.

  2 pounds of tomatoes, or 2 16-ounce
    cans of whole tomatoes, peeled

  4 cups vegetable broth or water

  1 large leek, cut in half lengthwise
    and chopped

  2 tablespoons olive oil

  1 carrot, chopped

  1 potato, peeled and chopped into
    1 inch pieces

  1 onion, chopped

  2 cloves garlic, chopped

  2 cups fresh basil leaves

  Salt and pepper to taste

Crush tomatoes in a bowl, retaining the juices. Chop all the vegetables and set in separate bowls. Charge the ingredients with your intent for love and romance, then begin cooking. Heat 1 tablespoon of the olive oil in a pot over medium heat. Add the onion, garlic, carrot, and potato. Cook for 5 minutes, stirring frequently.

Add tomatoes with the reserved juice, broth, and salt to taste. Bring to a boil; then reduce heat and simmer covered for 25 minutes, until vegetables are tender.

While the first part of the soup is cooking, wash the chopped leeks thoroughly. Heat the other tablespoon of oil in a pan. Sauté the leeks over medium heat for about 5 minutes, or until leeks are firm/tender. Remove from heat and set aside.

After the 25-minute cooking time is up, add the basil leaves to the soup and remove from heat. Purée soup with a stick blender or hand mixer until creamy, then add the leeks and season to taste. Return to heat and cook an additional 5 minutes to warm before serving.

Shopping List

Here is a list of the ingredients used in the recipes in this chapter.

❑ Allspice	❑ Cinnamon	❑ Mint (spearmint preferred)
❑ Apples	❑ Cloves	❑ Nutmeg
❑ Apple cider	❑ Coffee	❑ Olive oil
❑ Apricot jam	❑ Coffee creamer	❑ Onions
❑ Baker's chocolate squares	❑ Coriander	❑ Oranges

❏ Baking cocoa powder	❏ Eggs	❏ Oregano/ marjoram
❏ Baking powder	❏ Epsom salt	❏ Parmesan cheese
❏ Baking soda	❏ Ethyl rubbing alcohol	❏ Parsley
❏ Bananas	❏ Flour	❏ Potatoes
❏ Basil (fresh and dried)	❏ Food coloring (red)	❏ Salt (sea salt and regular)
❏ Black pepper	❏ Garlic	❏ Strawberries
❏ Black tea	❏ Ginger	❏ Strawberry jam
❏ Butter	❏ Honey	❏ Sugar (granulated, powdered, and brown)
❏ Candles (red, pink and blue)	❏ Ice cream (vanilla, chocolate, and/ or strawberry)	❏ Tomatoes
❏ Cardamom	❏ Leeks	❏ Vanilla extract
❏ Carrots	❏ Lemon	❏ Vegetable broth
❏ Chamomile tea	❏ Milk	❏ Wine (red)
❏ Chocolate sauce		

CHAPTER 8

Luck

There's nothing more annoying than feeling like you're wading through a run of bad luck. Everything just seems a bit off and like the world is against you. I assure you that it's not the case. "Bad luck" occurs when our intuition is distracted for whatever reason, and we are blocked from fully interacting with our inner guidance system. When this happens, we don't get that pull toward what is best for us, and we are left to flounder and flail in seeming chaos.

This can be caused by a number of different factors: exhaustion, excessive multitasking, illness, anxiety, and/or trauma can all contribute to a weakened connection to our inner voice. I don't mean to sound alarmist, but genuine psychic attack and black magic can also cause this bad luck problem; creating bad luck and misery is usually the goal of such acts. That being said, actual black magic that is directed toward you is rather rare, but if you feel this may be the case, work as many cleansings as you feel necessary to free yourself of any harmful energy before you work magic to restore your luck. Refer to chapter 3 for help in removing negativity.

The good news is that there are a great many options to magically improve your luck. After all, spells to improve your luck and good luck charms have been staples of magical practice for centuries.

Brews

These brews are a quick method of improving your fortune. They are a good first course of action to take if you are feeling stuck or blocked in your efforts, or if you are having trouble making a decision for fear of choosing incorrectly. The first is a surprisingly easy fruit juice drink.

Good Luck Juice Blend

4 cups of orange juice (preferably fresh, but concentrate will do in a pinch)

9 fresh strawberries

1 teaspoon vanilla extract

Wash, remove the stems, and mash the strawberries. Pour into a small pot and add the vanilla extract, warming over low heat to combine. Remove from heat and allow it to cool. Once cooled, combine the strawberry mixture with the orange juice, and charge with your desire to improve your luck. Pour the mixture through a sieve into a pitcher to remove any large chunks of strawberry (you can use the back of a spoon to mash more of the strawberries through the sieve). Drink a glass whenever you want to feel luckier and when making difficult decisions.

This next brew is a bit more expensive (about 16 dollars, last time I checked) due to its primary ingredient, but the investment is well worth it.

Golden Luck Brew

2 pinches saffron threads

2 cups water

Charge the saffron threads with your desire for luck, and place them in a pot with the water. Bring the water just to a boil and then remove the pot from heat. Once the brew has cooled, bottle and refrigerate it for future use. To use: Anoint the hands with the brew to enhance your luck or anoint good luck charms with a few drops of the brew to energize them. You can also sprinkle this brew in the corners of your home (if it won't stain your flooring) to create an atmosphere of good fortune.

Oils

What would a chapter on luck be without a nice, reliable luck-enhancing oil recipe? This recipe is easy to prepare and filled with ingredients that will bring positive energies into your life.

Good Luck Oil

1 tablespoon ground allspice

1 teaspoon grated orange zest

1 teaspoon powdered nutmeg

½ cup corn oil

Gently simmer the spices and orange zest in the corn oil until the scent is transferred. Remove it from heat and allow it to cool. Once the oil has cooled, strain it into a bottle, and charge it with your desire for good luck and happiness.

OIL SPELL
Bring Back My Luck Candle Spell

1 red candle

1 bottle of Good Luck Oil

A pin

Carve your name, birthdate, and astrological sign into the candle with the pin. Hold the candle in both hands, and charge it with your desire for improved luck. Anoint it with Good Luck Oil and light the candle. Say the following chant three times to seal the spell:

> *Misfortune and gloom are burned away;*
> *Good luck returns, here to stay.*

Allow the candle to burn out on its own if it is safe to do so. If not, let it burn for 15 minutes to an hour and extinguish with a candle snuffer. Relight it and repeat the chant daily until the candle has burned away.

Powder

This powder can be sprinkled in an automobile or boat to help ensure luck in your travels and proper decision-making while driving without it being too obvious that you are using magic. A little sprinkled under the driver's seat is usually sufficient. It can also be discreetly dispersed in the rooms of your home (if it can be done without ruining the flooring) to improve the home's luck and overall feel.

Good Luck Powder

1 tablespoon allspice

1 tablespoon nutmeg

1 tablespoon poppy seeds

1 tablespoon cornstarch

Charge each ingredient with the intention of luck, and grind each spice separately before combining them all with the cornstarch. Once the cornstarch has been added, bottle the completed powder. Dedicate it to the purpose of bringing good luck to you.

Charms

Good luck charms are well known even outside magical circles. From lucky horseshoes and rabbit's feet to special coins or herbs, a wide variety of things have been employed for centuries as charms in attempts to bring ourselves good luck. These days, we can create our good luck charms straight from the grocery store, no bunny feet necessary! In the following herbal charm, the element of fire is invoked to restore the connection and strength to your inner voice, bringing back your good luck.

Fiery Good Luck Charm Bag

1 part allspice

1 part basil

1 part rosemary

1 piece of dried orange peel cut in
the shape of an equal-armed cross

1 green cloth charm bag

1 green candle

Good Luck Oil

First, prepare the orange peel by cutting it into a small equal-armed cross shape and leaving it to dry out fully for several days. When the orange peel cross has dried and is ready, gather the rest of the ingredients and charge each of them with your desire for good luck. Fill yourself with a feeling of relaxed contentment, and transfer this feeling along with your desire into the candle and charm bag items.

Anoint the candle with a bit of the Good Luck Oil and light it. As the candle flames up, begin to add the herbs and orange peel cross to the cloth bag. When everything has been added, pour a drop of the melted green wax into the bag to seal the charm. Seal the bag. Once you've done so, hold the bag above the flame of the green candle, making sure to hold it high enough to avoid burning the bag or your hand, and consecrate it to its task with the following chant:

For good of all and by my free will,
Gentle promise, please fulfill.
Flame of Spirit; Ancient Fire,
Unlock within, my intuition.
Revive good luck and re-inspire
my higher mind connection.

Allow the candle to burn out on its own or snuff out the flame. Carry the charm bag with you, sleep with it under your pillow, and/or rub your third eye area with it daily for your luck to improve.

Red and Green Good Luck Charm

1 tablespoon dried chervil

1 tablespoon dried peppermint

Red charm bag

Combine the chervil and peppermint in a bowl and charge them with your intent. Pour the charged herbs into the charm bag and seal. Carry the bag with you at all times.

Foods

Food is always a good way to bring magical changes within. Since we are talking about good fortune, a process that starts within, food, like brews, is a quick method for creating improvement in your life. The following recipe is a light and healthy dessert and is great in summertime. Fresh fruit is rich in life energy, and these particular fruits are known to have positive "lucky" vibrations.

Turn Your Luck Around Fruit Salad

2 cups pineapple, cut into chunks

1 cup strawberries, sliced

2 oranges, segmented with the
membrane removed

Clean and prepare each of the fruits separately. Place each in a bowl and charge it with your intent to regain good luck, then combine the fruits in a larger bowl and mix. Eat as desired.

Lucky Green Persimmons

If you have a persimmon tree or know someone who does and want to increase your good luck, pick a green persimmon and charge it with your desire. Bury it in your yard to draw luck to you.

Witch Bottle

Witch bottles are a fun alternative to typical charms. Originally employed more than five hundred years ago as protective devices, witch bottles are now used for a wide range of magical intentions. They act as batteries of magical power and continue to radiate the energy of your intent as long as the seal remains unbroken. This witch bottle formula is easy to create, effective, and doesn't need to be carried around with you the way a charm does.

Capturing Luck in a Jar

9 persimmon seeds

1 tablespoon cinnamon, ground

1 teaspoon cloves, ground

1 teaspoon lemon zest or lemongrass

13 dried currants

Lock of your hair or nail clippings

2 tablespoons spearmint

1-2 cups water

Mason jar

Large red candle

Boil the water in a pot. Once the water is boiling, remove from heat and add the spearmint. Cover the pot and allow it to completely cool. While the water is cooling, place each of the first five ingredients in separate bowls, and charge them with your intent. When cooled, strain the spearmint water into a cup and light the red candle. Begin to assemble the witch bottle by adding each of the ingredients to the jar in the order given: persimmon seeds, cinnamon, cloves, lemon (zest or grass), currants, and your hair or nail clippings. Finally, pour the spearmint water into the jar. Make sure you have enough to fill up the jar. Put the lid on the jar and seal it by dripping red wax on the top and underside of the rim of the lid until it is completely covered in wax. Keep the bottle in a safe place. Whenever you feel the need for an extra boost, gently shake it to mix up the ingredients.

Shopping List

Here is a list of the items and ingredients used in this chapter.

❑ Allspice	❑ Currants	❑ Pins
❑ Basil	❑ Huckleberry	❑ Pineapple
❑ Candles (red and green)	❑ Lemon	❑ Poppy seed
❑ Chervil	❑ Lemongrass	❑ Rosemary
❑ Cinnamon	❑ Mason jar	❑ Saffron

❏ Cloth (red and green)	❏ Nutmeg	❏ Spearmint
❏ Cloves	❏ Orange (fruit and juice)	❏ Strawberry
❏ Corn oil	❏ Peppermint	❏ Vanilla extract
❏ Cornstarch	❏ Persimmon	

CHAPTER 9

Money

Money magic is wonderful for helping you out of those tight financial jams. Since money magic is usually only used when someone is low on funds, let's look for inexpensive ingredients for our money spells. There are loads of available ingredients which promote abundance, and they can help to bring extra money into your life when needed. Remember though that money itself is artificial and therefore has no endemic power.

One cannot "draw" money energy, for there is no such thing. The proper focus for money magic is on the energy and feeling of abundance and security; these are the qualities that money can bring. If you focus only on having a one hundred dollar bill in your hands, the spells will not be very effective. You must focus on the feeling of abundance and security, of not having to worry if the bills will get paid or if there will be money for food. Concentrate on the idea of already having that relaxed contentment—that what you truly need is being provided—when you cast a money spell, and you will draw prosperity to you like a magnet.

Oils

Aside from any uses in spellwork, these oils can be dabbed on money or worn on the body to encourage prosperity in your life. If worn on the body, anoint the wrists, third eye, and back of the neck, being sure to wipe off any excess.

Basic Money Oil

> 1 teaspoon allspice
>
> 1 tablespoon basil, dried
>
> 1 teaspoon chamomile (open up some chamomile tea bags)
>
> ½ teaspoon powdered cloves
>
> 1 teaspoon peppermint, dried
>
> ½ cup oil (sunflower preferred)

Simmer the herbs in the oil over very low heat until you can smell the herbs in the air. Allow to cool, strain, bottle, and charge with intent.

Money Now Oil

1 tablespoon cinnamon

1 tablespoon vanilla extract (or vanilla bean)

1 teaspoon peppermint, dried

½ cup almond or sunflower oil

A small piece of gold, silver, or pyrite
(optional)

Simmer the cinnamon and peppermint (and the cut-open vanilla bean, if used) in the oil over low heat until you can smell the aroma in the air. Remove from heat and allow it to cool. Once the oil has cooled, add the vanilla extract and the small piece of ore, if used. Charge the oil with your intent, and bottle for use. Note: Because the vanilla extract and oil will separate, it is necessary to shake the bottle each time before use. Vanilla bean makes a smoother product, but these are usually expensive and difficult to find in many markets. The extract is a perfectly fine substitute.

OIL SPELLS
Candle of Cash

1 bayberry-scented candle

Basic Money Oil

Cauldron or heat-proof dish

Small piece of paper (3 inches
square is ideal)

First, let's get a bayberry-scented candle—they're not too expensive. If you can afford it, you can buy an actual bayberry candle made from bayberry wax, but since these can be pricey, a scented candle can suffice. For now, scent counts more than color, so just get what you can (bayberry-scented candles are frequently red). For the spell, charge the bayberry candle with your intent and write the amount of money that you need on the fresh piece of paper. Anoint the corners of the paper with the money oil. Next, light the candle while holding the paper and chanting three, seven, or nine times:

Candle's flame, bring to me
The money that I need.

When you feel ready, light the paper in the candle's flame and set it in the cauldron or heat-proof dish to burn out. Your money should be on its way soon.

It Takes Money to Make Money Spell

1 green candle

1 gold candle

Basic Money Oil

Cauldron or censer

The highest denomination of paper money you have (a hundred dollar bill is excellent, if possible)

Arrange a money altar. One possible setup is to put the green candle on the left, the gold candle on the right, and the bottle of money oil and the paper money in the center. Relax and anoint the candles with the Basic Money Oil while charging them with your intent. Settle yourself before the altar holding the money while focusing on a feeling of prosperity and security. Infuse this feeling into the money and then set it on the altar between the two candles. Place each candle so it rests on the edge of the money, slightly touching it.

Next, anoint your third eye with the Basic Money Oil and focus your intent. When you feel ready, light the left, then right, candles while chanting:

Magic power, bring to me
Money and prosperity.

As the candles flame and glow, envision a beam of golden light streaming from your third eye into the money on the altar. See the money being filled with the golden light until you feel it can hold no more. When you think the money is full, dip the index finger of your dominant hand into the oil and place a dab of it onto the center of the bill to seal it and contain the golden light. Afterwards, you may extinguish the candles in the reverse order you lit them and end the ritual. Carry the money in a special place in your wallet or purse without spending it for as long as you can so it will draw prosperity to you.

Powder

Money Powder

1 tablespoon basil

1 teaspoon cinnamon

¼ teaspoon ginger

¼ teaspoon cloves

1 tablespoon cornstarch

Powder the herbs, and stir in the cornstarch. Empower the mixture with your intent, and bottle for use.

Powder Spell
Magic Change Purse

Green or gold-colored change purse

Money Powder

Paper money and a few coins

Place the paper money and the coins into the change purse and sprinkle some powder over the money. Close the change purse, hold it in both hands, and charge it with your desire. Keep it in a pocket, purse, or some place you keep other valuables in your home.

Charms

Money, Money, Come My Way Charm Bag

This spell is best cast outdoors or in a garage due to the smoke that is generated during the spell casting process.

1 green candle

Onion peels

Green cloth poppet

Money Now Oil

1 whole nutmeg

1 red cloth magic bag

1 silver coin (a silver-colored half-dollar coin or a quarter is a good, readily available choice)

Cauldron or heat-proof bowl

Soak the coin in saltwater for three days prior to the spell to cleanse it of any previous psychic energies or influences. For the magic charm doll (poppet), buy some green fabric or cut up an old green shirt that you no longer want to wear. Cut a large rectangle, then fold it in half. Next, cut that into a rough human shape (like a gingerbread man) so that you have two basic human shapes. Now, sew around the edges with green or gold thread to join the human shapes together, leaving a small opening at the head for stuffing. Use the outermost, papery onion peels to stuff the doll. Use as many peels as you need from as many onions as necessary, but only use the dry outer onion peels; the inner ones are too fresh. Once the doll has been fully stuffed, sew up the opening.

After the poppet is ready, arrange an altar with the cauldron in the center and the green candle placed behind it. The rest of the materials should be set in front of the cauldron. Anoint your wrists, third eye, and the back of your neck with the Money Now Oil. Anoint the candle and poppet with the oil and charge them each with your intent. Charge the nutmeg and coin as well. Now, light the candle and burn the poppet in the candle's flame, leaving it to burn to ashes in the cauldron. Once the ashes have cooled, pour them into the red charm bag along with the nutmeg and coin. Tie up the bag and anoint it with the Money Now Oil. Chant the following:

> *Money, money, come my way;*
> *Hurry forth without delay.*
> *Ease my burden and my stress;*
> *With abundance, I am blessed.*

Carry the charm bag with you wherever you go to speed money your way.

Foods

Bread of Plenty

1 envelope active dry yeast (quick rise is best)

2 tablespoons sugar

1 teaspoon salt

3 cups unbleached flour, plus additional
   for kneading

½ cup bulgur

½ cup wheat germ

2 cups hot water

A bit of oil

Sprinkle the sugar and yeast in a bowl along with 1 cup of the flour. Add the hot water (not too hot, just hot to the touch) and stir to mix. Set aside for five minutes. In a second bowl, combine the salt, 1 cup of flour, the bulgur and wheat germ. After five minutes, pour the yeast mixture into the dry mixture and stir to form a thick, gooey dough. Add the third cup of flour slowly while stirring to create a more solid dough. Knead on a floured surface, adding more flour as needed until dough is smooth and elastic in consistency. Form dough into a ball and place in a greased bowl, turning once to make sure the top of the dough is covered in a bit of oil. Cover with a towel or plastic bag. Allow to rise until doubled in size, approximately one hour. Punch down dough and divide into two balls. Grease two cookie sheets. Place one dough ball on each cookie sheet. Flatten the balls slightly to form a round loaf. Using a sharp knife, carefully cut a pentagram into the top of each loaf. Cover and allow them to rest for one hour before baking.

Ten minutes before baking, preheat the oven to 375 degrees. Bake the loaves for 25 minutes or until golden brown. Once the loves are baked, cool on wire racks and then bless both loaves. Hold your hands over it, sending energy and saying:

> *Gifts of earth, sown and reaped,*
> *Brought together for the feast.*
> *I offer in thanks for blessings bestowed,*
> *And ask for abundance to freely flow.*

Make sure the loaves are completely cooled before slicing. Reserve the first slice from each loaf to be buried in the earth with thanks.

Bath Salts

Money Bath Salt

3 cups Epsom salts

2 cups sea salt

1 cup baking soda

1 tablespoon (½ ounce) Money Now Oil

A few drops green food coloring

Mix the Epsom salt, sea salt, and baking soda together. Now, add the oil a few drops at a time, being careful not to add too much. Remember, it should have a consistency like damp sand, not oily salt-soup. Once you have added enough oil, put a few drops of green food color in and mix.

The bath salt should come out looking light green. Once made, the bath salt should be charged to bring abundance to anyone who uses it. To use, add ¼ cup to ½ cup to a warm bath and relax in the water, soaking in the energy of prosperity. When soaking in the tub, it is a good idea to mediate on the idea of being financially secure and happy.

Witch Bottles

This witch bottle invokes the powers of the four elements to draw security and abundance to you. Each ingredient corresponds to one of the classical elements of earth, air, fire, and water.

Elemental Money Bottle

1 Mason jar

Basic Money Oil

¼ cup whole wheat kernels or unbleached, whole wheat flour (earth)

¼ cup long grain brown rice (air)

¼ cup flax seeds (fire)

4 chamomile tea bags (water)

5 coins of the same worth (highest denomination available)

1 green candle

Soak the coins in saltwater for three days to cleanse them of any prior influences, and then rinse them clean in fresh water. When you are ready, anoint the green candle with the Basic Money Oil, in addition to your wrists, third eye, and back of the neck. Charge the candle with your intent. Next, layer the ingredients in the jar in the order given: wheat, rice, flax seeds, and chamomile (break open the tea bags and sprinkle the contents into the jar). Push each coin into the layers of grains, seeds, and flowers, holding it vertically and pushing it down through the layers like a coin in a vending machine. Place them at the five pentagram points in the jar.

Once the coins have been added, close the jar tightly. Using the green candle, drip wax over the top of the lid to seal it. Finally, hold the jar in both hands and charge it with energy. Chant the following:

Earth, air, fire, water—
In this jar, together merge.
Elements of life, join your power;
Prosperity and abundance does now surge!

Leave the jar on a table where you can see it, and leave your purse or wallet near the jar whenever possible.

Shopping List

Here's the list of ingredients used in the spells and recipes in this chapter.

❑ Allspice	❑ Cornstarch	❑ Rice (brown)
❑ Almond oil	❑ Epsom salt	❑ Salt (sea salt and regular)
❑ Baking soda	❑ Fabric (green and red)	❑ Sugar
❑ Basil	❑ Flax seeds	❑ Sunflower (oil and seeds)
❑ Bulgur	❑ Flour (unbleached)	❑ Vanilla extract
❑ Candles (green, gold, and bayberry-scented)	❑ Food coloring (green)	❑ Wheat germ
❑ Chamomile tea	❑ Ginger	❑ Whole wheat kernels (or whole wheat flour)
❑ Cinnamon	❑ Mason jar	❑ Yeast
❑ Cloth (red and green)	❑ Onions	
❑ Cloves	❑ Peppermint	

CHAPTER 10

Protection

Magical protection is a very important subject. I don't want to sound paranoid, but there are so many scary people in the world. It is therefore a good idea to protect ourselves in as many ways as we can. Using a magical form of protection does not give us permission to be reckless, however. No matter how magically protected you may be, never leave your doors unlocked or your windows open at night thinking that *only* magic will keep you safe. Magic is very powerful, but if you ask for trouble, trouble is going to try to find you. It might not be able to harm you right now, but why create a situation where you have to maintain overwhelming eternal vigilance? Always use common sense and mundane safety measures whenever possible. Magical protection can be used as an added advantage, but it can't be your only defense. Now that my rant is over, let's look at some simple protective measures you can take.

Brews

Salt has been used in ceremonies for centuries; its protective and cleansing qualities are well attested. There is, however, a secret to using salt effectively. That secret…is water. The explanation behind salt's protective and cleansing abilities is that it helps to diminish unwanted electrical and psychic energies. By itself, salt is usually not enough, as it does not conduct electricity (nor is water by itself.) When they are combined, however, something magical occurs, and saltwater becomes a conductor of electricity. So, to be optimally effective magically, salt and water must be combined. Many people do not know this, and choose to use them separately with diminished results. I have heard about many people salting their windows for protection, but it won't be as effective as possible if water isn't included. To get the most out of your salt, it must be combined with water either as saltwater or at least as dampened salt.

The snag with using saltwater is that it dampens and dries salt out. Once it has dried, its effects are again diminished. If you wish to use salt as a protective tool, it is a good idea to make a large batch of saltwater and charge it with protective energy. Then pour it into small glass or ceramic bowls or cups, and place one in each room of your home. You will have to check every so often for evaporation. When it happens, add some freshly made and charged saltwater.

Protection Potion

Another option for basic protection is to brew a protection potion. A protection potion can be made from the following items:

2 cups water

1 sprig of rosemary

1 sprig of peppermint

1 sprig of parsley

1 small pinch of salt

Brew these ingredients into a "tea." When it has cooled, charge it for protection and keep it in a glass bottle. To use the protection potion, sprinkle it on doors and windows and anoint yourself with it as if it were an oil or perfume. This potion offers portable personal protection that's less noticeable than an amulet. You can sip a little bit of it to infuse yourself with protective energies, but it doesn't taste all that great—it's green and salty!

Oil

The following oil can be worn on the body for personal protection; you can anoint your wrists, third eye, and the back of your neck. It can also be used to anoint candles used in spellwork or objects (if safe to do so without damaging) that you wish to be protected from harm or theft.

Protection Oil

> 1 tablespoon basil
>
> 1 tablespoon oregano
>
> 1 tablespoon sage
>
> ½ cup vegetable oil

Pour the oil and herbs in a pot and heat over low heat until you smell the herbs in the air, then remove from heat. Allow the oil to cool completely and then strain it into a jar. Charge the oil with your intent for protection.

Powder

Protection powder can be sprinkled around the outside of the home to offer protection to its occupants, as well as in cars or around objects you wish protected. It can also be poured into a black or red charm bag and carried as an amulet of protection.

Protection Powder

> 1 teaspoon basil
>
> 1 teaspoon bay leaves
>
> 1 teaspoon oregano
>
> 1 teaspoon peppermint
>
> 1 teaspoon sage
>
> ¼ teaspoon black pepper
>
> 1 tablespoon cornstarch

Grind the herbs together into a powder. Stir in the cornstarch to bind them all together, then bottle and charge the mixture with your desire for protection.

Charms

If you want to make simple and effective protective amulets, there are some options.

Rosemary Wreath

> 3 fresh rosemary sprigs
>   (the longer, the better)
>
> White thread
>
> Black thread

Take the three fresh rosemary sprigs and tie the stems together at one end with white thread, then begin to braid the stems together until you reach the end. When you have finished braiding, tie the other end together with black thread. Lastly, tie both ends together in a loop with the same thread. Charge the sprigs as an amulet of protection and hang it in your home, either in the kitchen or over the front door.

Autumn Gourd Wards

Gourds have protective abilities, and they are easy to find in stores for use as decorations in autumn. Turning them into protective wards to guard your home is a perfect subtle means of magical protection. You can set some in each room, and everyone will think they are ordinary decorations for the season. You will need:

Several gourds, any variety

Braided black three-strand cord of natural
fiber (cotton, wool, etc.; yarn works well)

Large altar-table or altar cloth (big enough
to set all the gourds on)

2 white candles in sturdy holders

Your cord will need to be long enough to be tied in a loop and placed around all the gourds in a circle. Place the altar cloth on the floor or use a table. Set the cord loop on the altar space. Place all the gourds within the loop. Set the candles at the back of the altar space, one on each side. Settle yourself in front of the altar space and light the candles. Close your eyes, and visualize yourself and your working area encased in a glowing orb of electric blue energy. See this energy extend around you in a circle large enough to work in. When ready, open your eyes and hold your hands over the gourds. Sweep your hands over the gourds in a clockwise circle and send energy into them, visualizing that they are being joined together with white light like a magical chain. Chant this spell:

Autumn gourds with hardened shell,
Linked as one to guard me well.
Join together, form a shield;
Protection power you now wield.

Now you can place a gourd or two (or more) in each room of the home and even intermingle them with other decorations.

Foods

One handy (if stinky) item you should always have on hand is the onion. These vegetables have the ability to absorb negativity, and if you suspect that your home is haunted, you can place two halves of a cut onion in the suspected center of the haunting—the room in which you feel the most uneasy. Leave the onion there for at least twenty-four hours. If the onion begins to weep and ooze (instead of drying up), it is a sign of negative spiritual energy and haunting. A word of warning: this procedure will result in the room smelling *very* oniony. The air will be stinging to the eyes. Afterwards, it is a good idea to thoroughly air out the room.

Some foods can be eaten to alter your body's energy and give you a stronger aura of protection. Some good choices include chili (beans, garlic, onions, and peppers are strongly protective), blackberries and blueberries, and corn.

Following are some recipes that incorporate these ingredients.

Protection Shield Chili

2 cups 13-bean soup mix (or your favorite dried beans), soaked overnight in water

1 cup onion, chopped

1 bell pepper, chopped

2 garlic cloves, minced

¼ teaspoon cumin, ground

1 tablespoon oil

1 teaspoon oregano

1-2 tablespoons chili powder

1 teaspoon salt

½ teaspoon black pepper

1 tablespoon light brown sugar

2 cups tomato (or spaghetti) sauce

Rinse and strain the beans and place in a large pot with fresh water. Boil beans until tender (usually 1 to 2 hours), adding more water if needed. Meanwhile, sauté the bell pepper, onion, and garlic in a pan with the tablespoon of oil until very soft. Then, add the seasonings, stirring to combine. Remove from heat. When the beans are tender, drain any excess liquid and add the sautéed onion, garlic, and pepper mixture to the beans. Now add the tomato sauce and stir to combine. Simmer on medium heat for 10 minutes. Remove from heat. Hold your hands over the pot (high enough to avoid steam burns), and move them in a clockwise circle while sending your energy and intent for protection into the chili while saying this spell:

Gifts from earth, this precious food;
When eaten, the protection energy is
 Released and revealed.
The magical energy now imbued
And charged to strengthen my spiritual shield.

It is now ready to serve.

Blackberry and Blueberry Blend

1 pound fresh blackberries

1 pound fresh blueberries

2 teaspoons sugar, granulated

Rinse the berries thoroughly. Next, toss them with the sugar in a bowl. Place your hands over the bowl and move them in a clockwise circle over the fruit while sending your energy and desire for protection into them. Chill for at least 2 hours to allow the berries to absorb the sugar before serving.

Roasted Corn on the Cob

2 to 4 ears of corn, fresh

Butter, 2 tablespoons per ear of corn

Peel back the husks on the ears of corn and remove as much of the corn silk threads as you can. Rinse in water to remove any dirt or loose bits of corn silk. Rub each ear with about 1 tablespoon of the butter; it is easiest to just rub the stick of butter on the corn. Fold the corn husks back up over the ears and charge each one with your desire for protection. Wrap each ear individually in aluminum foil and place on a pan in a 400 degree oven or on a barbecue grill, and roast for 25 minutes. Serve with an additional tablespoon of butter.

Witch Bottles

Though witch bottles (also known as spell bottles) have been used for protection and sending negative energy back to its source for centuries, the original recipes for their construction usually contain some unsavory or dangerous ingredients. Urine and mercury—among other things—aren't the healthiest items to be working with, so newer, more modern formulae have been created over the years which are equally effective without the unpleasantness. The following witch bottle is quick to create and very effective.

Protection Spell Bottle

> 5 sprigs fresh rosemary
>
> 2 cups water
>
> 5 garlic cloves
>
> 9 straight pins
>
> Lock of hair or fingernail clippings
>
> Mason jar
>
> 1 black or red candle (whichever
>   color feels more powerful to you)

In a pot, heat the water to just boiling, then remove from heat and toss in the rosemary. Cover and let stand until it has completely cooled. Once the rosemary infusion has cooled, you may begin. Light the candle. Place the garlic, straight pins, and lock of hair and/or nail clippings in the jar, along with the rosemary sprigs from the pot. Next, carefully pour the rosemary infusion into the jar over the rest of the ingredients.

Secure the lid on the jar tightly. Hold the jar in both hands while focusing on a feeling of safety and protection. Send white light from your hands into the jar until it feels full. Now pick up the candle and carefully drip wax all over the jar lid until it is completely covered, in order to seal the spell. Once the lid is covered, hold the jar in both hands again and say:

> *Witch's bottle of herbs and pins,*
> *Absorb and pierce harm sent to me.*
> *Protect me now from evil and danger,*
> *And as I will, so mote it be.*

Take the jar and hide it somewhere in the home, bury it in the ground, or place it beneath the bricks of the hearth. These are the traditional places to leave the bottle to do its work.

Shopping List

❏ Aluminum foil	❏ Cloves	❏ Peppermint
❏ Basil	❏ Cords, black (yarn or twine)	❏ Onion
❏ Bay	❏ Corn	❏ Rosemary
❏ Bean soup mix (13 bean)	❏ Cornstarch	❏ Sage
❏ Bell pepper	❏ Cumin	❏ Salt
❏ Blackberries	❏ Dill	❏ Straight pins
❏ Black pepper	❏ Garlic	❏ Sugar (granulated and light brown)
❏ Blueberries	❏ Gourds	❏ Thread (white and black)
❏ Butter	❏ Marjoram/ oregano	❏ Tomato sauce
❏ Candles (white, black, and red)	❏ Mason Jar	❏ Vegetable oil
❏ Chili powder	❏ Parsley	

CHAPTER 11

Psychic Ability and Divination

There are many foods, potions, and methods for enhancing the psychic ability that lies dormant in most of us, just waiting to be unleashed. Fortunately for the modern-day practitioner, a large amount of ingredients that can promote psychic ability are just waiting for us at the supermarket. The trick, of course, is in knowing what to look for and combine to create the desired effect. Since this chapter is about both enhancing psychic ability and divination, I will include a few simple divination methods using these ingredients, all of which I have found to be effective.

Brew

Magical brews to enhance psychic ability go way back in both fact and fiction. From Welsh legends of the goddess Cerridwen and the potion she was brewing in her cauldron—of which Taliesin consumed a bit and gained knowledge, magic, and psychic ability—to Shakespeare's *Macbeth*—in which the three witches brew up a potion to cause spirits to reveal knowledge—making magical brews for psychic enhancement is well known as a magical skill. Luckily, we don't have to stir the brew for a year or add eye of newt for our brews to work. The following potion is quick, simple, and effective.

Psychic Enhancer Potion

> 1 teaspoon anise seeds
>
> 1 teaspoon peppermint
>
> 1 teaspoon tarragon
>
> ¼ teaspoon cinnamon
>
> ⅛ teaspoon cloves
>
> 2 cups water

Bring the water just to boiling and remove from heat. Add the herbs and spices, and cover. Allow to steep for ten to fifteen minutes. Lift the lid and charge the potion with your desire for enhanced psychic ability. Strain into a cup and sip slowly while engaging in divination work.

Powder

This powder can be sprinkled around dark blue or purple candles to enhance their ability to boost your psychic potential. It can also be carried in a charm bag as a personal talisman to enhance your psychic power, and it can be used in divination.

Psychic Powder

> 2 tablespoons cinnamon
>
> 1 tablespoon nutmeg
>
> 1 tablespoon cloves
>
> 1 tablespoon peppermint
>
> 1 tablespoon lemongrass
>
> 2 tablespoons cornstarch

Grind all the herbs together and stir in the cornstarch. Charge with your desire and pour in a jar for safekeeping.

Powder Spell
Powder Divination

> ½ cup Psychic Powder
>
> 1 white candle
>
> Reading surface (something disposable like a piece of cardboard)
>
> Large bowl

Light the white candle and allow melted wax to build up. When there is plenty of melted wax, drip some wax in a random pattern on the cardboard. Set aside the candle. Sprinkle the powder over the wax and then gently pick up the cardboard and shake the excess powder into the bowl. Now, look at the cardboard and search for any symbols, letters, numbers, or words. Interpreting these is a personal matter of discovering what they mean to you, although consulting a book on tea-leaf reading is always helpful.

Dream Pillow

Breathing in the scent of magical herbs and absorbing their energies while you sleep is a wonderful way of unlocking your psychic potential. An herbal pillow is the best means of accomplishing this. The following pillow is easy to create.

Prophetic Dreams Pillow

Cloth napkin, small pillowcase,
   or two 5-inch squares of fabric
   (white, dark blue, or purple)

Needle and thread (white,
   dark blue, or purple)

4 tablespoons bay leaves, crumbled

4 tablespoons chamomile

4 tablespoons peppermint

4 tablespoons thyme

4 tablespoons anise seed

1 tablespoon lemongrass

Stuff the pillowcase (or sew up three sides of the cloth squares or napkin and stuff) with the herbs and sew up the end. Charge the pillow with your desire for prophetic dreams. Sleep with this pillow on top of your regular pillow to induce psychic dreams.

Oil

This oil can be worn on the body or used to anoint candles used in spells designed to increase your overall psychic ability, or on candles used during divination.

Psychic Oil

2 teaspoons thyme

1 tablespoon lemongrass

¼ teaspoon cloves

½ cup olive oil

Warm the herbs and oil in a pot over low heat until you can smell the herbs in the air. Remove from heat and allow it to cool completely. Charge the oil with your intent for enhanced psychic ability, then strain and bottle for use. Cloves can be irritating to the skin, so they can be omitted if desired, but I recommend including them. Years ago, I read a recipe for an herbal charm for psychic ability using cloves as its primary ingredient. Skeptical, I tried it and was surprised at its effectiveness. There is something about cloves that seems to awaken the mind.

OIL SPELL
Water Scrying

> Cauldron or black bowl
>
> Water
>
> Psychic Oil
>
> 2 dark blue or purple candles

Fill the cauldron or bowl three-quarters of the way full with water. Anoint the candles with the oil. Use the oil to anoint your third eye, wrists, and back of the neck as well. Place the candles far enough behind the cauldron so that their flames are not reflected into the water when you are gazing. Light the candles. Calm and center yourself and gaze into the water. Relax your vision and continue to gaze. This may take a few attempts, but after a while the water will appear to cloud over and images will form. Interpret the symbols according to your personal reactions.

Food

There is one food that can be used in an easy and time-honored method of divination: eggs. The egg has been employed to determine whether or not a pregnant woman will have twins by rubbing it on her belly and then cracking it open to see if there is one yolk or two. Studying the condition of the yolk can also provide clues as to the baby's health; a rotten egg or bloody yolk are ill omens. There is also a method of scrying using an egg and water, and it is quite simple to perform.

Ovamancy

1 egg

1 clear bowl of water

Crack the egg into the bowl of water and study the shapes that the egg whites take in the water. Look for signs and omens. Again, these should be interpreted according to your own intuition, but consulting a book on tea-leaf reading could be helpful.

Charm

A handy magic charm relating to psychic ability is a pendulum. A pendulum can be easily made using a nut and some thread. In Irish lore, the hazel is considered the tree of wisdom. Its nut, the hazelnut or filbert, is packed with wisdom-enhancing energy; using one as a pendulum can help you find the answers you seek.

Pendulum of Knowledge

1 hazelnut

White thread

1 sturdy needle

Carefully take the needle and poke a hole through the center of the hazelnut. This may take more than one try so it is a good idea to buy several nuts and take your time. Once you have the hole through the center, take the thread and feed it through the hole. Tie a knot in the thread so that you basically have a bead on a string. Cut the thread to about 12 inches. Charge the pendulum with your intent that it be a divinatory device and will always tell the truth. It is ready for use.

Pendulum Divination

To use the pendulum, hold the end of the string between the thumb and forefinger of your strong hand and ask the pendulum to give you its answer for yes. It will swing. Note the pattern of this swing. It may be back and forth or in a circle. If a circle, it may turn in a clockwise circle or counterclockwise circle. No matter how it moves, note that it is the pendulum's "yes" motion. Now ask it to indicate its no response. Note the swing of the pendulum this time. Once you have clear indications of yes or no answers, you may begin to ask questions. The swing will indicate the answers to your questions. Take clear notes at all times so you remember what was asked and what the answers were. This will give you a way to gauge accuracy as you progress.

Witch Bottle

This spell bottle can be created to be a continual force of psychic-enhancing energy channeled to you.

Psychic Spell Bottle

   1 tablespoon anise seed

   1 tablespoon celery seed

   1 tablespoon flax seeds

   1 tablespoon mace (or nutmeg)

   3 bay leaves

   Bottle or Mason jar

   1 dark blue or purple candle

   Psychic Oil

Anoint yourself and the candle with the Psychic Oil. Light the candle. Place each of the herbs into the bottle and close the lid tightly. Hold the bottle in both hands and charge with your intent of increased psychic ability. Drip melted wax over the lid until it is completely covered to seal the spell. If possible, keep the bottle by your bed so you can absorb its energies while you sleep.

Shopping List

Here is the list of ingredients used in this chapter.

❏ Anise	❏ Cloth (white, dark blue, or purple)	❏ Needle
❏ Bay	❏ Clove	❏ Nutmeg
❏ Bottle or Mason jar	❏ Cornstarch	❏ Olive oil
❏ Candles (white, dark blue or purple)	❏ Eggs	❏ Orange
❏ Celery seeds	❏ Flax seeds	❏ Peppermint
❏ Chamomile	❏ Hazelnuts	❏ Tarragon
❏ Chicory	❏ Lemongrass	❏ Thread (white, dark blue or purple)
❏ Cinnamon	❏ Mace	❏ Thyme

CHAPTER 12
Sabbats and Esbats

All witches know the importance of the sabbats (solar and seasonal holidays) and the esbats (lunar celebrations and non-sabbat gatherings), and that each one has a different form, focus, and feel to it. These holidays are a witch's way of keeping connected to the rhythm of the universe, but they are also more than this; depending on tradition, each sabbat (and sometimes, each esbat) has a rich history of ritual observance delving deep into the myths of that particular culture. Given how varied the sabbats and esbats can be, I will mostly speak of them in general and basic terms. There are many different things created for each of the holidays, such as oils, incenses, powders, brews, and foods. It would be redundant to include tons of food recipes for the different holidays, but I will include a few. The main focus of the food sections is on lists of ingredients and food ideas for the different holidays, which you can combine in your own way for your holiday feasts.

The sabbats are celebrated eight times a year in the following order:

- Samhain (SOW-en), October 31

- Yule (yool), around December 21

- Imbolg (IMM-olg), February 1

- Spring Equinox, around March 21

- Bealtaine (bee-el-TIN-nah), May 1

- Summer Solstice, around June 21

- Lughnasadh (LOO-nasa), August 1

- Autumn Equinox, around September 21

Please note that each of the sabbats is known by many variant names (again, depending on tradition), but these are fairly common names and how I address them on the following pages. I focus on each sabbat individually and follow up with a section on esbats. For now, let us begin at the beginning. For witches, Samhain marks both the ending and the beginning—our new year.

Samhain

This holiday is generally celebrated on October 31 and is the main origin of the secular holiday of Halloween. In the old calendar, Samhain marks the beginning of the dark half of the year, the third harvest. This period is the meat harvest, the opening of the veil between this world and the otherworld, and a time to honor the dead. Even though these may seem like bleak or spooky reasons to mark a holiday, this night is always celebrated with joy and is usually a favorite day of witches. In many traditions, this night also honors the crone goddess, and many Witches pay homage to her on this night. I myself honor the crone goddess Cailleach (KYLE-ee-ock) on Samhain, for it is said that at this time she is reborn and begins summoning forth the powers of winter. She is the ancient Celtic hag goddess of winter and a possible derivative of the green-faced "witch" so prominent in modern Halloween decorations today. She has a blue-black face; the old Scottish word *glas* referred to the color blue-black in some instances, but green in others, so it has been suggested that a mistranslation may have led to "witch hags" being given green faces. The word *cailleach* is still used today to refer to a witch. That being the (possible) case, I have made my peace with the green-faced witch and have decided to add her to my own Samhain/Halloween decorations with the intention of honoring the Cailleach.

Other modern Halloween customs also find their origins in the distant past. Costumes, jack-o'-lanterns (originally and sometimes still made of turnips), apple bobbing, ghost stories, and even trick-or-treating all have historical and Pagan significance. I personally choose to revel in the secular side of Halloween before I have the formal Samhain ritual later that night. Celebrating the modern, public side of Halloween helps lend that feeling of tribal acknowledgement of the day to my Samhain experience. When these festivals were first celebrated in ancient times, everyone in the community, and indeed everyone in Celtic (and other) nations, acknowledged and usually took part in the rites. These days, newer religions have pressed the Pagan holy days into the shadows and they are only celebrated by small, spread-out groups with little public fanfare. Through the mask of Halloween, Samhain has luckily retained a large public presence. Even though non-Pagans usually do not have any idea of the holiday's true significance, the energy of so many people all participating in one of our holidays leaves me with a wonderful feeling of community.

On this night, it is traditional to release the energy of the old year, honor the dead, honor the crone goddess, ask for protection through the dark half of the year, work divinations to foretell events in the new year, and make a wish for the future. There are many ways to do these things and I will give a few examples. For divinations, the methods described in chapter 11 can be used as part of your Samhain celebration.

Brew

Special brews to help you embrace the energies of the season can be created for each of the sabbats. These are known as attunement teas. One example is the following:

Samhain Attunement Tea

¼ teaspoon allspice

4 cups apple cider

¼ teaspoon sage

⅛ teaspoon cloves

Warm the apple cider in a pot to just under boiling and add the herbs. Remove from heat and cover. Allow to steep for ten to fifteen minutes before straining and drinking. As you drink it, focus on letting go of the past (the old year) and connecting to the future.

Powder

This powder can be sprinkled in circles around the altar candles to enhance your attunement to the power of this day during your ritual.

Samhain Powder

1 tablespoon sage

1 tablespoon tarragon

1 teaspoon cloves

1 tablespoon cornstarch

Grind and mix the herbs together and then combine with the cornstarch. Charge the powder with your intent to connect with the energy of Samhain; focus on the feeling you get as Halloween draws near and infuse this into the powder.

Powder Spell
Making a Samhain Wish

> 1 small piece of paper
>
> Pen
>
> 1 apple
>
> Samhain Powder
>
> Knife
>
> Paper bag

Write out your wish on the piece of paper. Cut the apple in half through the center and sprinkle the Samhain Powder over the pentagram shape that is exposed on the inside of the apple halves. Fold the paper into a square, making sure to make all folds toward you. Place the paper on the bottom apple half and set the other half of the apple on top. Carefully put the apple in the paper bag and twist up the bag to secure. Hold the bag in both hands and focus all your energy and intent on achieving your goal. Bury the bag with the apple in it to seal the spell.

Oil

You can use this oil to anoint the body prior to ritual, or to anoint candles used in Samhain rites.

Samhain Oil

    5 hazelnuts, crushed

    1 tablespoon rosemary

    2 teaspoons tarragon

    ½ cup olive oil

Warm the olive oil, hazelnuts, and herbs in a pot over low heat until you can smell the herbs in the air. Remove from heat and charge them with the energy of Samhain; keep the image of gently falling autumn leaves and the feeling this image evokes as you send energy into the oil. Strain and bottle the oil for use.

OIL SPELL
To Honor the Crone

    1 black candle

    Samhain Oil

Anoint the candle with the oil and charge it to be a sacrifice in honor of the crone goddess. If you are honoring a specific goddess, charge the candle to be a sacrifice in her honor. As you light the candle say the following:

> With this candle I now light,
> I honor you on this sacred night.
> Mighty Goddess, queen of the dark;
> Into your season, I now embark.

Please guide me on my spiritual path,
And protect me from harsh winter's wrath.
Blessed be.

Charms

Charms of protection are traditional during this time of greater connection to the Otherworld. Even though we invite the spirits of our loved ones to our celebrations, it is still a good idea to have protective amulets to prevent any unwelcome spirits from making their presence known. The first and most obvious charm of protection used on this night is the jack-o'-lantern.

Jack-O'-Lantern

Originally made from hollowed-out turnips with a candle placed inside, modern jack-o'-lanterns are hollowed-out and carved pumpkins. Whether using a turnip or pumpkin, the principle of the lantern remains the same: to turn away evil.

1 large pumpkin

1 sharp knife

Black marker (optional)

Candle (preferably black or orange)

It is traditional to carve a scary looking face on the jack-o'-lantern to scare away any nearby evil, but you can also carve runes, pentagrams, or other symbols of protection instead of a face, or incorporate it into the face's design. After settling on a design, draw it on the front of the pumpkin with the marker so you have a pattern to follow while carving. Once you've hollowed out the middle, carve the pumpkin and bless it as an amulet of protection. Use a blessed candle to light up the pumpkin.

No-Ghoul Garlic

This charm is very easy to create; you only need one ingredient!

Rope of garlic bulbs

The protective powers of garlic have been known for centuries. Nearly everyone has heard that garlic repels vampires, but regardless of whether or not that is true, garlic is indeed quite a strong magical protectant. Charge a rope of garlic with protective energy and hang it in your kitchen. You can also make several and add them to your Halloween decorations to keep evil at bay. You can also carry a single garlic clove in a black magic charm bag as an amulet of personal protection.

Foods

There are many foods that are traditional and modern that can be eaten in celebration of the holiday. Since Samhain marks the third harvest, the meat harvest, foods that contain beef, pork, or other meats are traditional. Breads are also traditional, as are foods made from squash, turnips, potatoes, and corn. While it is true that potatoes are definitely *not* ancient in Ireland, they have been grown there since the sixteenth century, so they have been traditional fare for a considerable amount of time. Here are some recipes and ideas for Samhain.

Apple bobbing

Basin of water

Several apples

For luck in the new year, it is traditional to eat an apple on Samhain night. If the apple can be plucked out of the water without using your hands, it is even luckier. Fill a large basin with water and float several apples in the water. Everyone can take a turn trying to grab an apple with their teeth. Whoever gets their apple the fastest should have the best luck of the year.

Apple Spirit Food

It is a traditional practice to bury apples in the earth so that their energies can feed those spirits wandering about on this night.

Dumb Supper

It is an Irish Samhain tradition to set extra places at the table for departed loved ones to honor them, and to eat the dinner in silence, hence the name "dumb" supper. Traditional foods for this supper include porridge, bread, wine or mead, and a bit of tobacco set on the table. These days, we are free to enjoy many foods at our dumb supper. I personally have never liked porridge, but to each their own.

Samhain Stew

2 pounds of beef stew meat

1 large onion

1 garlic clove, minced

1 teaspoon salt

2 cups carrots, sliced

4 medium potatoes cut into chunks

1 turnip, cubed

¼ cup corn kernels

1 medium zucchini, sliced

4 bouillon cubes

3 cups water

⅓ cup flour

⅓ cup olive oil

Cut the meat into 1 inch cubes. Lightly dust the meat in a little flour. Brown the meat a few pieces at a time in a large sauce pan. When all the meat has been browned, set it aside and place the onions and garlic in the pan, cooking until onion is tender (about 3 to 5 minutes). Add the rest of the flour, and while stirring constantly, add water until smooth. Add the bouillon and salt. Add the meat back to the pan and heat until boiling, stirring constantly. When it has begun to boil, reduce heat to low and allow to simmer for 2 hours, stirring occasionally and adding a little water if needed. Add the rest of the vegetables, except zucchini. Heat to boiling again and then reduce heat to low and simmer for another 20 minutes. Finally, stir in zucchini and simmer for 10 minutes, until the zucchini is tender. Serve hot.

Shopping List

Here is the list of the ingredients used in the Samhain section.

❑ Allspice	❑ Corn	❑ Potatoes
❑ Apple (fruit and cider)	❑ Cornstarch	❑ Pumpkin
❑ Bay	❑ Flour	❑ Rosemary
❑ Beef (stew meat)	❑ Garlic	❑ Sage
❑ Bouillon cubes	❑ Hazelnut	❑ Salt
❑ Candles (black)	❑ Olive oil	❑ Tarragon
❑ Carrots	❑ Onion	❑ Turnip
❑ Cloves	❑ Pork	❑ Zucchini

Yule

Yule, Nollaig, Winter Solstice—whatever you wish to call it, it is a magical night. Give or take a few days, December 21 marks the point at which winter begins in the northern hemisphere; it is the day in the earth's orbit when the sun is directly over the tropic of Capricorn and we receive the least amount of the sun's rays. This is the low point in the solar cycle (for the northern hemisphere; for those in the southern hemisphere, it is the summer solstice at this time), but it is also the point of beginning anew. Though this day is the shortest of the year, from this point forward, the days will become longer and the sun's influence will grow in strength. It is for this reason that it's said the sun is reborn on this night.

Many Pagan practices used to celebrate Yule were adopted into Christianity's Christmas holiday; everything from Santa to presents to the Christmas tree are actually Pagan in origin and are perfectly suited to our Winter Solstice sabbat festivities. To celebrate this time of solar rebirth, many candles are lit to symbolize the light of the sun returning to us; boughs of evergreen are brought indoors to reinforce our connection to nature and to bring its life force into our homes; a yule log is lit in honor of the heat of the sun; and a feast is held to celebrate both surviving the harshness of winter and the hope of things to come.

Brew

Wassail is an excellent "attunement tea" for Yule. There are quite a few variant recipes for this drink, many with alcohol. I have chosen to include a nonalcoholic version that is easy to prepare and very effective for attuning to the spirit of the season.

Nonalcoholic Wassail

½ gallon apple cider

2 cups orange juice

½ cup lemon juice

1 ½ teaspoons pumpkin pie spice

2 tablespoon sugar

Cinnamon sticks or candy canes

Combine all ingredients in a large pot. Simmer over low heat for 30 to 45 minutes, stirring occasionally. Remove from heat and charge with intent to connect with the Yuletide spirit. Serve in mugs with a cinnamon stick or candy cane.

Powder

Yule Powder

1 teaspoon cinnamon

1 teaspoon nutmeg

½ teaspoon cloves

1 teaspoon chamomile

1 tablespoon cornstarch

Grind all the herbs together and add the cornstarch. Charge the powder with intent and bottle for use.

Powder Spell
Yule Pine Cones

This charm enhances the holiday atmosphere without being as overpowering as those store-bought, spice-scented pine cones.

Pine cones

Old paintbrush

Water-based glue

Yule Powder

Water

Disposable bowl

Large pan

Pour some glue into the bowl and dilute slightly with water; stir with the paintbrush. Paint the ends of each pine cone with the glue. Holding the pine cone over the pan, sprinkle the pine cone with the powder, shaking off any excess. Allow the pine cones to dry, and then charge them with your desire to enhance the holiday atmosphere. Once dried, you can decorate with them as you would any other pine cones.

Oil

Yule Oil

>1 tablespoon rosemary
>
>Peel from one apple
>
>¼ teaspoon cinnamon
>
>½ cup sunflower oil

Add the oil, cinnamon, apple peel, and rosemary to a pot; heat over low heat until you can smell it in the air. Remove from heat and allow it to cool. Charge with your desire, strain, and bottle for use.

Oil Spell

It is part of Yuletide to welcome back the reborn sun. One way to do this is through candle magic.

Welcoming the Sun

>1 white candle
>
>Yule Oil
>
>Pin

Carve a sun shape (a circle with eight spokes) onto the candle, and then anoint it with the oil. Charge the candle with solar energy and light it. Chant the following:

From longest night to bright new day,
The sun is reborn and I rejoice.

Gaze at the candle for a bit and focus on the return of the waxing light.

Charm

Since Yule is filled with magic, it is only natural that some of the items we commonly associate with this time of year started out as charms.

Tree Ornament

It is said that the glass ball ornaments seen on Christmas trees are descended from the protective charms known as witch balls. It's quite easy to turn an ordinary glass ornament into a witch ball.

1 large round hollow glass ornament

1 tablespoon rosemary

Carefully remove the loop for the ornament hook, and fill the opening with the rosemary. Replace the loop and gently hold the ornament in both hands to charge it with your intent for protection through the winter. Hang on your Yule tree where it can radiate its energy throughout the home.

Foods

The Yule feast menu is usually similar to what people eat for Christmas dinner: roast turkey or pork, stuffing, vegetables, cookies, pies, and one of my favorites, mashed potatoes.

Yuletide Mashed Potatoes

Potatoes are healing and nurturing foods, both in their regular use and in their magical abilities. Butter is symbolic of transformation and is a sacred food of the fae, as is milk. Combining these foods creates a classic comfort food perfect for the holiday.

6 medium potatoes, cubed

¼ cup butter

¼ teaspoon black pepper

1 ½ teaspoons salt

½ cup milk

In a large pot, boil potatoes until very tender, 30 minutes. Drain the potatoes and place in a large bowl. With a large fork or hand mixer, mash the potatoes, adding the milk, salt, and pepper until smooth and creamy. In modern times, it is a wise idea to substitute 1% milk for whole milk and to use a fat-free butter substitute when making mashed potatoes; though butter is symbolic of transformation, the physical transformation we undergo from eating too much of it is usually unwelcome!

Shopping List

Here is the list of items and ingredients used in the Yule section.

❏ Apple (fruit and cider)	❏ Glue	❏ Pine cones
❏ Black pepper	❏ Lemon juice	❏ Potatoes
❏ Butter (or fat-free butter alternative)	❏ Milk	❏ Pumpkin pie spice
❏ Candles (white)	❏ Nutmeg	❏ Rosemary
❏ Chamomile	❏ Orange juice	❏ Salt
❏ Cinnamon	❏ Ornaments	❏ Sugar
❏ Cloves	❏ Paintbrush	❏ Sunflower oil
❏ Cornstarch	❏ Pins	

Imbolg

Though Imbolg is one of the major sabbats of the year, its traditional practices are rather few due to the fact that it falls in one of the coldest parts of the year for many. This sabbat marks the "quickening of the year"—a time to work divinations to foretell the weather and see if frost is out of the ground. This is an important holiday in the agricultural sense for it is the turning point in the year (halfway between winter and spring) and it is hoped that early planting may begin at this time or soon after, weather permitting. It is also an important holiday in the religious sense because in the old days, it was celebrated by many as the day of Brigid, a powerful fiery goddess of inspiration and smithcraft. In the modern craft, it is seen as a celebration of the recovery of the goddess from her work in giving the sun rebirth.

Due to its weather forecasting element, Imbolg has filtered down into modern society as Groundhog Day, the day when people observe a groundhog to determine if winter is waning or if it will last six more weeks. Anciently, it was noted that if serpents came out of their holes at this time or if frogs could be heard croaking, the ground had thawed and it was likely that warmer days were on their way. The more modern use of a groundhog seems to be divination by opposites. If the groundhog sees its shadow (meaning the day has to be somewhat sunny for there to be a shadow), it is said to mean that winter shall remain cold for another six weeks. If the groundhog does not see its shadow (since on cloudy days there are rarely shadows), it means that winter is ending early. Rather than observing snakes or frogs or sneaking up on cute little groundhogs, I prefer to use other divination methods for predicting the weather and what the future may hold in the coming spring.

Brew

The attunement tea for Imbolg combines the energy and warmth of the sun with the cozy closeness of the remaining winter.

Imbolg Attunement Tea

2 chamomile tea bags

¼ teaspoon sage

3 cups water

1 tablespoon honey

½ teaspoon lemon juice

Heat the water to boiling, then remove from heat. Steep the tea bags and sage for five to ten minutes. Next, pour a cup of the tea, adding the honey and lemon to the cup. Sip to connect with the energy of the holiday.

Powder

Imbolg Powder

1 tablespoon sage

1 tablespoon chamomile
  (about two tea bags worth)

1 tablespoon cornstarch

Grind the herbs together and stir in the cornstarch. Charge with your intent to connect to the energy of Imbolg. Bottle the powder for use.

Powder Spell
Brigid's Spell for Strength

 1 red candle

 Imbolg Powder

 Pin

Using the pin, carve an upward-pointing triangle into the candle. Charge the candle with your desire for inner strength both in health and in overall willpower. Sprinkle a ring of Imbolg Powder around the base of the candle and light the candle. Say the following chant:

> *Power of fire; candle's flame,*
> *Restore my strength in Brigid's name.*

This may be repeated for as long as desired. Allow the candle to burn for as long as is safe.

Oil

Imbolg Oil

 1 tablespoon chamomile

 1 tablespoon sage

 1 teaspoon coriander

 ½ cup almond oil

Warm the oil and herbs over low heat until you can smell the herbs in the air. Allow to cool and charge with the fiery energy of Imbolg. Bottle for use.

OIL SPELL

Oil Scrying

Imbolg Oil

Small black bowl

Pour the oil into the bowl and gaze into it for omens and symbols of the future.

Foods

Lamb is a traditional food of Imbolg, as are dairy foods and all edible seeds.

Roast Leg of Lamb

3 juniper berries (optional, if available)

2 teaspoons mustard

¼ teaspoon black pepper

2 teaspoons salt

15 pound leg of lamb

Preheat oven to 325 degrees. Crush the juniper berries (if using) and stir them in with the mustard, salt, and pepper. Spread the mustard mixture all over both sides of the lamb. Place the lamb with the fat side up on a rack in a roasting pan. Roast for 2 to 2 ½ hours until meat has internal temperature of 160 degrees on a meat thermometer.

Charm

Seeds are packed with the growth and abundance energy of Imbolg, sunflower seeds in particular. Using seeds and grains in a prosperity charm now maximizes effectiveness as we begin the time of waxing light.

Seeds of Prosperity

1 tablespoon sunflower seeds

1 tablespoon brown rice

1 tablespoon poppy seeds

1 green cloth magic bag

Charge the seeds and grains with your desire for prosperity and place in the magic bag. Seal the bag and hold it in your hands. Chant the following as many times as you feel necessary to seal the spell.

Seeds and grain, sprout abundance;
Bring prosperity to me now.

Carry this charm with you as much as possible.

Shopping List

Here is the list of ingredients used for Imbolg in this section.

❏ Almond oil	❏ Garlic	❏ Mustard
❏ Black pepper	❏ Green fabric	❏ Poppy seeds
❏ Candle (red)	❏ Honey	❏ Rice (brown)
❏ Chamomile tea	❏ Juniper berries	❏ Sage
❏ Coriander	❏ Lamb Leg (15 pound)	❏ Salt
❏ Cornstarch	❏ Lemon juice	❏ Sunflower (oil and seeds)

Spring Equinox

The Spring Equinox celebrates balance. The sun is perfectly over the equator, day and night are equal, and we've arrived at the midpoint between winter and summer. Flowers bloom in a burst of color and life. The sweet songs of birds fill the blossoming trees and the earth herself feels young, renewed, and revived. Even those of us with really strong allergies can still appreciate the beauty of this magical time…at least once the allergy medicine kicks in. It is such an awe-inspiring sight to see bees, butterflies, and birds all working to complete nature's cycle, pollinating flowers and cracking open seeds.

This time of year can offer great opportunities for connection to nature and appreciation of the delicate balance and how each creature has an important part to play.

Again, if you suffer from allergies make sure that you have the appropriate medication with you as necessary. Gasping and wheezing tend to be a distraction from communion with nature—this I know for a fact.

On the Spring Equinox, it is traditional to celebrate new life and the growth of nature in its waxing cycle. Traditional practices include coloring eggs as symbols of fertility, decorating with flowers and herbs, and eating fresh early fruits and vegetables in the sabbat feast.

Brew

The attunement tea for the Spring Equinox is a bright mix of herbs.

Spring Tonic

1 tablespoon marjoram/oregano

1 tablespoon thyme

1 tablespoon peppermint

2 cups water

Honey (optional)

Heat the water to just boiling then remove from heat and add the herbs. Cover the pot and allow the herbs to steep for 10 to 15 minutes. Sweeten with honey if desired.

Oil

Spring Equinox Oil

1 tablespoon marjoram/oregano

1 tablespoon tarragon

1 teaspoon thyme

½ cup sunflower oil

Put the herbs and oil in a pot and heat on low until you can smell the herbs in the air. Remove from heat and allow to cool. Charge the oil with your intent, strain, and bottle.

Oil Spell

Spring Cleaning Besom

A besom is a witch's ritual broom. It is used for purification and cleansing magic. You can enchant a regular broom with magic and use its power to cleanse your home of negativity.

1 broom

Spring Equinox Oil

Anoint the handle of the broom with a dab of the magic oil. Wipe off any excess so the handle is not too slippery and gently sweep each room of the house in a clockwise motion to clean out the psychic grunge that builds up over time. When you are finished, wash the whole broom in cold running water.

Powder

Spring Equinox Powder

  1 tablespoon lemon zest, dried

  1 tablespoon thyme

  1 tablespoon cornstarch

Grind together the lemon zest and thyme, then stir in the cornstarch. Charge with your intent and bottle.

Powder Spell
Springtime Energy Boost

  1 pink candle

  1 yellow candle

  1 light blue candle

  Spring Equinox Powder

Set the pink candle on the back left corner of an altar table. Set the light blue candle on the back right corner, and set the yellow candle in the front middle of the table to create a triangle pointing at you. Sprinkle a small ring of powder around each candle. Sit before the table and light the candles in this order: pink, blue, then yellow. Say this chant to focus the spell:

> *As flowers begin to bloom and grow,*
> *The world is blessed with waxing light.*
> *I ask for renewed energy to flow, and*
> *Restore my strength, vigor, and might.*

Sit before the candles in quiet meditation for a while to soak up their energy. When finished, extinguish them in reverse order of lighting.

Charms

Eggs are a traditional feature of this holiday, as they symbolize growth and fertility. The practice of coloring eggs dates back hundreds of years. You can use decorated eggs as charms to bring in the energies of the season and place them among your other ordinary decorations without anyone being aware of their magical purpose.

Eostre Eggs

12 hard-boiled eggs

Food coloring or water-based paint

Several small cups to hold the coloring

White vinegar

Spoon

Wire rack

If using the food coloring, pour the coloring into the cups and add a ¼ teaspoon of vinegar to each cup. Lower an egg into each cup. Allow the eggs to soak up the color for fifteen minutes, then remove to wire rack to dry. Once the eggs have dried, hold each one and charge it with your desire for it to become a charm of springtime energy.

Seeds of Magic

Planting magically charged seeds in the ground and then cultivating the plant that develops is an excellent way of utilizing the growth-related energy of this time in manifesting your desires. Plant seeds of an herb or flower that corresponds magically to your goal. You can look at the shopping lists at the end of each chapter to find herbs that magically relate to your goals.

1 packet of seeds (from a plant
   aligned with your magical intent)

1 cup of blessed fresh water

Flower pot or seed starter tray

Potting soil

Pack the potting soil into the flower pot or seed trays. Bless the water to be free of all impurities. Open the seed packet and pour all the seeds into your strong hand. Will your energy into the seeds and charge them with your desire. Carefully plant a few seeds in each tray or spread out the seeds in the flower pot. Chant this spell as you sprinkle the blessed water over the seeds:

This is my aim, this is my goal;
[State goal] will manifest for me as you grow.

Make sure to tend to the seeds and water them regularly. Transplant them to your garden after a few weeks, and nurture them to maturity.

Foods

The foods of spring are any early fresh fruits and vegetables, eggs, and mixed greens.

Quick Spring Soup

3 large potatoes, diced

2 large carrots, sliced

1 cup macaroni noodles

1 zucchini, sliced thick

2 cups tomato (or spaghetti) sauce

2 teaspoons thyme

2 teaspoons oregano

1 teaspoon salt

1 teaspoon sugar

4 cups water

Add all ingredients except tomato sauce in a pot and boil until the vegetables are tender. Add the tomato sauce and simmer until thickened slightly. Serve warm.

Shopping List

Here are the ingredients used in the Spring Equinox recipes.

❏ Black pepper	❏ Lemon	❏ Sugar (granulated)
❏ Broom	❏ Macaroni	❏ Sunflower oil
❏ Candles (pink, yellow, light blue)	❏ Marjoram/ oregano	❏ Tarragon
❏ Carrots	❏ Packet of seeds	❏ Thyme
❏ Cornstarch	❏ Peppermint	❏ Tomato sauce
❏ Eggs	❏ Potatoes	❏ Vinegar (white)
❏ Food coloring or water-based paint	❏ Potting soil	❏ Zucchini
❏ Honey		

Bealtaine

The May Eve/May Day sabbat is the counterpart to Samhain/Halloween. Where Samhain initiates the dark half of the year, Bealtaine brings in the light half of the year and the full force of nature's power. On both holidays, the veil between this world and the Otherworld thins, and spirits and faeries roam the night. In the modern craft, this day is seen as the mating/wedding of the Goddess and God.

Brew

Bealtaine is a time of flowers and herbs, bees and honey, growth and greenery. The attunement tea for this holiday draws this energy.

Bealtaine Attunement Tea

1 hibiscus tea bag

1 passionflower tea bag

1 peppermint sprig

Honey (optional)

2 cups water

Heat the water to boiling and remove from heat. Add the peppermint and the two tea bags. Allow to steep for 10 minutes and pour a cup. Sweeten with honey if desired.

Oil

This oil can be used to anoint candles for growth spells and Bealtaine rituals. It can also be used to anoint the body for Bealtaine and to encourage strength.

Bealtaine Oil

1 tablespoon marjoram/oregano

1 tablespoon coriander

Pinch paprika

½ cup almond oil

Heat the herbs and oil on low until you can smell the scent in the air. Remove from heat and allow to cool. Once cooled, charge the oil and bottle for use.

Powder

This powder can be sprinkled around the candles on your Bealtaine altar during rituals to increase your ability to connect with the energy of the holiday.

Bealtaine Powder

1 tablespoon marjoram/oregano, dried

2 teaspoons cilantro, dried

1 teaspoon curry powder

1 teaspoon paprika

1 tablespoon cornstarch

Grind and mix the herbs together, then add the cornstarch. Charge the powder with your intent, and bottle for use.

Charms

Most of the magical work of Bealtaine centers around fertility and growth. Any of the fertility spells and recipes in chapter 6 can be used at this time for an extra boost of power. Here is a way to charm a plant to encourage it to grow.

Charmed Plant

During Bealtaine, it is wise to bless plants for growth. If you have a garden and want to bless it subtly, you can bless one plant indoors and plant it in your garden with the intent that the blessing will spread to all the other plants.

> 1 small potted plant (tomato, zucchini, or whatever is available)
>
> Cauldron or large bowl
>
> 1 besom (or regular broom anointed with a bit of Bealtaine Oil)

Set the plant in the cauldron and place the cauldron in the middle of the room, on the ground. Focus your intent while holding the besom, lightly sweep a clockwise circle around the cauldron, and plant with the intent of cleansing the plant of any negativity or ill health. Finally, hop over the plant on the broom (seriously!) and state with conviction, "I bless this plant and the earth!" Now you can plant it in the garden and as you do, visualize it growing strong and healthy. Affirm in your mind that this blessing shall spread to all the plants in your garden.

This blessing is reminiscent of ancient crop blessings in which people leapt high in the fields astride poles to bless and encourage plant growth. That practice is one of the origins of the belief that witches fly on brooms, which is partially why I recommend doing it indoors to avoid developing an odd reputation amongst your neighbors.

Foods

Any and all fruits and vegetables are appropriate for Bealtaine, but especially strawberries. Their rich red color and sweetness capture the vibrancy of this time of year. Early grains are also appropriate; oat cakes are the ancient traditional food eaten at this time.

Bealtaine Oat Cakes

¾ cup oatmeal

½ cup flour, plus extra

¼ teaspoon salt

½ cup water

2 tablespoons vegetable oil

Mix together the dry ingredients, then stir in the water. Mixture will be sticky. Knead the dough on a floured surface, adding flour just until the dough is no longer sticky. Press dough into a circle a ¼ inch thick. Cut the circle into eight wedges. Add the oil to a pan and cook each wedge on medium-high heat until browned on both sides; 3 to 5 minutes per side. Remove to a cookie sheet. Once all the wedges are cooked, place them in a 250 degree oven for ten minutes or so to make them crisp. Serve with butter and strawberry jam.

Shopping List

Here are the ingredients used in the Bealtaine section.

❏ Almond oil	❏ Flour	❏ Passionflower tea
❏ Butter	❏ Garden plant	❏ Peppermint sprigs
❏ Cilantro	❏ Hibiscus tea	❏ Salt
❏ Coriander	❏ Honey	❏ Strawberry jam
❏ Cornstarch	❏ Marjoram/ oregano	❏ Vegetable oil
❏ Curry powder	❏ Oatmeal	
❏ Flax seed	❏ Paprika	

Summer Solstice

The first day of summer (around June 21 in the northern hemisphere) marks the time when the earth is at a place in her orbit where the sun is directly over the tropic of Cancer, and the northern hemisphere receives the largest amount of sunlight. In the southern hemisphere, the summer solstice is around December 21, when the sun is directly over the tropic of Capricorn. The summer solstice is the longest day and is the counterpart to the winter solstice—the longest night. It is a time for celebrating the high point of the solar cycle, protecting crops and animals through this time of continued growth, and honoring the power of fire, especially for its cleansing and protective qualities.

Brew

The midsummer attunement tea contains parsley, sage, rosemary, and thyme, but I'm not breaking out into song. These herbs just have an affinity for the summer season and help us better connect to its energy.

Midsummer Attunement Tea

> 1 tablespoon rosemary
>
> 1 tablespoon thyme
>
> 1 teaspoon sage
>
> ½ teaspoon parsley
>
> 2 cups water

Heat the water to boiling, then remove from heat. Add the herbs, cover, and allow it to steep for at least ten minutes. Strain and sweeten with honey if desired.

Oil

This oil can be worn on the body or used to anoint candles during midsummer celebrations to better connect with the energy of this day. This oil can also be used for cooking midsummer meals to bring the summer energy within.

Midsummer Oil

1 tablespoon basil

1 teaspoon sage

1 teaspoon chives

1 teaspoon chervil

½ cup sunflower oil

Combine oil and herbs in a pot and heat over low until you can smell the scent in the air. Remove from heat and allow the oil to cool. Charge the oil with your intent to capture the energy of summer. Strain and bottle the mixture for use.

Powder

It should be noted that this powder recipe does not contain any cornstarch. The reason for this is that the spell that follows requires the burning of the powder and burned cornstarch smells weird. If you are using this powder to circle candles or for any other noncombustible purpose, you can add 1 tablespoon of cornstarch, as it does a good job of holding the powder together.

Midsummer Powder

1 tablespoon basil

1 tablespoon thyme

1 tablespoon sage

Grind and combine the herbs, and charge them with your intent.

Powder Spell

This spell is done to offer thanks to the gods, to ask that disease be kept from us, and to ask that we flourish and prosper though the summer. If you have a garden, ask also that the plants continue to thrive and that the harvest will be bountiful.

Midsummer Sacrifice

Midsummer Powder

Small bonfire

If you have an outdoor fire pit, it would be ideal to have a midsummer gathering or barbecue and light a fire in the fire pit for this spell. You could also use a cauldron on the ground outdoors with a small fire kindled within it, or even a cauldron indoors with a candle in it. Light the fire (in whichever form), pick up the container of powder, and focus on your desire for blessing. When you are ready, toss the powder into the fire (or sprinkle a bit on the candle's flame) with the words:

> *Mighty gods of summer's glory,*
> *I offer these herbs in sacrifice.*
> *May disease be kept far from me,*
> *And through the summer may I thrive.*
> *Blessed be.*

Charm

This charm captures the energy of midsummer and confers luck, protection, and abundance to its wearer if you keep these qualities in mind as you create the charm bag.

Midsummer Charm Bag

 1 teaspoon dried corn seeds

 1 teaspoon fennel seeds

 1 teaspoon wheat kernels
  (or whole wheat flour)

 1 teaspoon sunflower seeds

 1 tablespoon dried rosemary

 1 yellow, gold, or green charm bag

Combine the seeds and herb in a bowl or cauldron and charge them with your desire. Pour the mixture into the charm bag and seal it. Wear or carry it as often as possible to keep the powerful energy of the Summer Solstice with you until the next sabbat.

Foods

The foods of summer are barbecue, fresh salads, and fruit. Here's a salad recipe that's light and perfect for this time of year.

Midsummer Salad

> 1 head of lettuce (any type), shredded
>
> 2 medium tomatoes, chopped
>
> 1 medium zucchini, grated
>
> 4 mushrooms, sliced
>
> ½ cup baby spinach leaves, shredded or torn

Dressing

> ½ cup Midsummer Oil
>
> 2 tablespoons plus one teaspoon
>   apple cider vinegar
>
> ½ teaspoon salt

Combine and toss the salad ingredients. Mix the ingredients for the dressing in a bottle with a tight-fitting screw top. Shake the bottle vigorously for a minute or so to combine the vinaigrette dressing. Pour dressing over the salad and toss once more before serving.

Optional: If desired, you can add ¼ cup sunflower seeds and/or ½ cup of shredded cheese and 1 cup cubed chicken breast that has been sautéed in 2 tablespoons oil and 1 teaspoon minced garlic.

Shopping List

Here is the list of ingredients used in the Summer Solstice section.

❏ Apple cider vinegar	❏ Garlic	❏ Shredded cheese
❏ Basil	❏ Lettuce	❏ Spinach (baby leaves)
❏ Chervil	❏ Mushrooms	❏ Sunflower (seeds and oil)
❏ Chicken breast	❏ Peppermint	❏ Tarragon
❏ Chives	❏ Parsley	❏ Thyme
❏ Cloth (yellow, gold, or green)	❏ Rosemary	❏ Tomato
❏ Corn seeds	❏ Sage	❏ Wheat kernels (or whole wheat flour)
❏ Fennel seeds	❏ Salt	❏ Zucchini

Lughnasadh

This holiday marks the beginning of the harvest season and is celebrated as the first festival of harvest. Lughnasadh is the origin of the county and state fairs we have today. Anciently, large gatherings were held for trade, horse racing, games, and feasting, all in celebration of the harvest as well as for commerce and preparation for the coming winter. It is the time of year to take stock and evaluate whether or not you have what you need to make it through the dark half of the year.

For most of us, the fear of actually completely running out of food, water, or firewood before springtime with no way to get more is no longer a reality, but it is still wise at this time to make sure you are prepared and that everything is in order to get through the winter months. Modern concerns that can be addressed at this time include finances, auto and home repairs, and any insurance needs as well as the traditional concerns regarding food, animals, water, and firewood. None of this is meant to imply that Lughnasadh is a boring holiday; far from it. It is a night devoted to feasting, games, honoring the earth goddess and god, and working sympathetic magic to cool the heat of the sun. This magic is worked in order to prevent the often-scorching August heat from damaging the crops before they can be fully harvested.

Brew

The attunement tea for Lughnasadh isn't so much a tea as it is a juice blend. Since this sabbat marks the beginning of the harvest, berries and apples are perfect choices to help us connect to the energy of the day, as they are just beginning to reach their peak.

Lughnasadh Juice Blend

1 cup blackberry or raspberry juice

1 cup apple juice

Mix the two juices together and sip slowly while focusing on the power of the sun.

Oil

Lughnasadh Oil

1 teaspoon pearl barley

1 tablespoon grated apple peel

3 dried mushrooms (any edible variety)

1 crushed hazelnut

¼ cup sunflower oil

¼ cup corn oil

Heat the oils and other ingredients in a pot over low heat until you can smell the scent in the air. Remove from heat and allow the oil to cool. Charge the oil with intent. Strain and bottle for use.

Oil Spell

This spell is designed for the positive people, things, and experiences in your life. It is both a show of appreciation for these things and also a call for their protection and preservation in your life.

Lughnasadh Spell for Preserving Blessings

1 white candle

1 black candle

1 yellow or gold candle

Pin

Pen and piece of paper

Lughnasadh Oil

Anoint the candles with the oil. Set the black candle on the left side of the table and the white candle on the right. Carve a sun symbol (a circle with eight rays coming from it) in the yellow candle and place it in the center of the table. Next, take the pen and paper and write out a blessing list: names of people, things, and experiences for which you are grateful and would like to preserve. Anoint the blessing list with Lughnasadh Oil by dabbing a bit on each corner. Set it under the yellow/gold candle. Now light the black candle and say:

> *Goddess, eternal one, sovereign origin of creation, you who never wane but merely change your focus: please preserve the wondrous gifts you have bestowed upon me. I am truly grateful for all you have given me and pledge my vigilance in caring for my blessings.*

Light the white candle and say:

> *Mighty God, you who have provided abundance for all your children and whose cycle of life, death, and rebirth shall be mirrored by us all: I ask you grant the continued existence of and connection to my blessings. I give my thanks and pledge my lasting appreciation for what I have been given.*

Light the yellow/gold candle and say:

Power of the sun, golden, fiery orb, empower the blessings in my life with continued strength and protection. Blessed be.

Allow the candles to burn for as long as you can, then extinguish in reverse order of lighting, with thanks.

Powder

This powder can be used not only in Lughnasadh celebrations but also in prosperity magic.

Lughnasadh Powder

   1 tablespoon cornmeal

   1 tablespoon whole wheat flour

   1 tablespoon rye flour

   1 tablespoon cornstarch

Combine the cornmeal, flours, and cornstarch. Charge with your intent, and bottle the powder for use.

Powder Spell
Harvest Money Spell

   1 green candle

   1 yellow or gold candle

   1 piece of whole grain bread

Butter

Lughnasadh Powder

Charge both candles: the gold candle to bring in the power of the sun, and the green candle for the energy of the earth. Set the green candle on the left and the gold candle on the right of your altar. Pour a ring of powder around each candle. Light the candles. Spread the butter on the whole grain bread, and with your finger charge the bread with intent by focusing your energy and tracing a sun symbol in the butter. Fold the bread in half to capture the sun symbol within and say:

> *The power of the sun and power of the earth have here conjoined to give form to abundance. I have in my hands the gift of harvest. I partake of the harvest so that I may reap my own prosperity. So mote it be.*

Eat the bread and butter to take the energy of abundance into yourself.

Charm

A good charm for this holiday is the making of a corn husk doll. You can buy corn husks in the store; tamales are wrapped in them.

Lughnasadh Corn Doll

Corn husks

If the husks are too dry to work with, you can soak them in water for a little while to make them more pliable. Twist the corn husks into a roughly human shape. Make a loop for the head and twist arms and legs. You can bless the corn husk doll as a symbol of abundance and keep in the home until the next Imbolg, when it is then buried in the garden.

Foods

The foods of Lughnasadh are the first harvest gleanings—nuts, berries, squashes, breads, beans, and also lamb. Corn has also become a main staple of food at this time, so here is a recipe for cornbread.

Lughnasadh Cornbread

> 1½ cups cornmeal
>
> 1 cup unbleached flour
>
> 2 teaspoons baking powder
>
> 4 tablespoons sugar
>
> ¾ teaspoon salt
>
> 2 large eggs
>
> 1 cup milk
>
> 4 tablespoons butter

Preheat oven to 450 degrees. Grease a square baking pan with butter. In a mixing bowl, beat the eggs and add the butter, milk, flour, cornmeal, sugar, salt, and baking powder until well blended. Pour batter into pan and bake 20 to 25 minutes. Allow to cool and cut into eight pieces.

Shopping List

Here are the ingredients used in the Lughnasadh section.

❏ Apple (fruit and juice)	❏ Cornstarch	❏ Pearl barley
❏ Baking powder	❏ Eggs	❏ Rye flour
❏ Blackberry juice (or raspberry juice)	❏ Flour (unbleached)	❏ Salt
❏ Butter	❏ Garlic	❏ Sugar
❏ Candles (white, black, yellow or gold, and green)	❏ Hazelnut	❏ Sunflower oil
❏ Corn (meal and oil)	❏ Milk	❏ Whole grain bread
❏ Corn husks	❏ Mushroom	❏ Whole wheat flour

Autumn Equinox

The second festival of harvest is a time of giving thanks for the bounty of the earth. This holiday is often known as the "Witches' Thanksgiving," a name that is very appropriate.

The Autumn Equinox is the true time of thanksgiving, as late November is well past harvest season.

Now that the blazing heat has cooled and the leaves are beginning to change, we return to a time of balance. The day and night are equal once more, as this day is the dark twin to the Spring Equinox with the sun positioned directly over the equator. The Spring and Autumn Equinoxes would be identical but for the fact that one is on the upswing and the other is on the downswing of the year. The Autumn Equinox is the beginning of nature's period of rest; the focus of the life energy of plants shifts more to their roots, versus the rush of energy needed in spring to create and sustain new flowers and green leaves.

The majority of the celebration of this sabbat involves giving thanks to the mother goddess for earth's bounty and also drawing the remaining light and heat of the sun into our bodies and into the earth to help sustain us through the time of darkness. If we were comparing the sabbats to the lunar phases, the Autumn Equinox would be the last quarter moon before the dark-moon time of Samhain. On this equinox, we celebrate the mother goddess, as this is the time when she is beginning to transform into the crone. It is a bittersweet festival of giving thanks and releasing anything holding us back so we are ready to journey into the unknown at the new year.

Brew

The attunement "tea" for the Autumn Equinox is a blend of harvesttime juices and herbs that serve to connect us to the energy shift.

Autumn Tonic

> 2 cups apple juice
>
> 1 cup pomegranate juice
>
> 1 passionflower tea bag
>
> 1 teaspoon sage
>
> Honey

Heat the apple juice to just under boiling, then remove from heat and add the sage and tea bag. Allow to steep for ten minutes. Add the pomegranate juice and reheat if you want it warm, or stir in honey to taste and drink.

Oil

This oil carries with it the energies of the harvest—falling leaves, cool breezes, longer nights, and that cozy feeling of fall. It can be used in spells for wisdom and protection as well as in the sabbat celebration.

Autumn Equinox Oil

> 1 tablespoon rosemary
>
> 1 tablespoon apple peel

2 hazelnuts, crushed

½ cup almond oil

Combine all ingredients in a pot and heat over low until you can smell the scent in the air. Remove the pot from heat and allow to cool. Once cooled, charge the oil with intent, strain, and bottle it for use.

Oil Spell

This spell is a rite of pure thanksgiving. It transmits your gratitude to the goddess and god.

Autumn Rite of Giving Thanks

1 dark red candle

1 brown candle

1 orange candle

1 yellow candle

1 green candle

Autumn Equinox Oil

Anoint all the candles with the Autumn Equinox Oil and place them in a semicircle on the table, starting with the dark red candle on the left and moving forward with the brown, orange, yellow and finally the green candle on the right. Light the candles from left to right, saying:

The earth begins her time of slumber;
For my blessings, I give thanks to you.
My heart and mind are filled with wonder;
The gifts of harvest shall see us through.
My loyalty and heart you have always and forever;
My devotion is eternal, ceasing never.
Blessed be.

Allow the candles to burn for as long as possible in sacrifice to the goddess, and then extinguish them in reverse order of lighting.

Powder

This powder can be used for protection of home and property, as well as used in the sabbat celebration.

Fall Harvest Powder

> 1 tablespoon rosemary
>
> 1 tablespoon sage
>
> 1 tablespoon autumn leaves,
>   dried and crushed
>
> 1 tablespoon cornstarch

Grind and combine the herbs and leaves. Then add the cornstarch. Charge with your intent and bottle the powder.

POWDER SPELL
Circle of Protection
Fall Harvest Powder

Pour a ring of powder around the outside of your home to bless and protect it from danger.

Charm

This charm can be made to increase wisdom and the ability to make correct choices, and all it takes are three nuts that are renowned for their powers of wisdom and mind-strengthening.

Autumn Nut Charm

1 black, brown, or red charm bag

1 almond

1 hazelnut

1 walnut

Charge each of the nuts individually with your intent, then place them in the charm bag and seal it. Carry the bag with you as often as possible.

Foods

The foods of the Autumn Equinox are all the traditional Thanksgiving foods: roast turkey or chicken, mashed potatoes, baked squash, apple and pumpkin pies, and breads.

A traditional bread for the sabbats is an older, heavy bread known as bannock.

Harvest Bannock

> 2 cups flour
>
> ½ teaspoon salt
>
> ½ cup butter
>
> ½ cup water

Mix together the flour and salt. Cut in the butter and add water. Knead the dough until smooth. Grease a pan (preferably cast iron) and press the bannock into the pan. Bake on top of the stove on low heat. Cook slowly, making sure the outside does not burn before the center is cooked. When the bread can be released from the pan (about ten minutes into cooking), carefully flip it over and cook the other side of the bread, approximately ten more minutes. Place on wire rack to cool. Bless the bread as it cools, and serve with butter.

Shopping List

Here are the items and ingredients used for Autumn Equinox in this section.

❑ Almond (nuts and oil)	❑ Cornstarch	❑ Pomegranate juice
❑ Apple (fruit and juice)	❑ Flour	❑ Rosemary

❏ Butter	❏ Hazelnut	❏ Sage
❏ Candles (dark red, brown, orange, yellow, and green)	❏ Honey	❏ Salt
❏ Cloth (black, brown, or red)	❏ Passionflower tea	❏ Walnut

Esbats

Esbats are celebrations held on specific moon phases. The full moon is a common time to hold an esbat, but they may also be held on the new moon or on a weekly basis. Weekly coven meetings aren't usually overly formal; they are generally study meetings, so I am going to focus on the new moon and full moon esbats.

New Moon Esbats

The new moon is the time when the sun and the moon meet in the same astrological sign and are considered "conjunct," and if there is an exact conjunction, a solar eclipse results. Since the new moon is the beginning of the lunar cycle, a new moon esbat is a time of new beginnings. In my tradition, any meetings held on the new moon focus on asking for guidance and inspiration to understand the nature of our obstacles and the strength to overcome them. Then the chalice (filled with juice or wine) and a white candle are passed around and each member gives thanks for a blessing in their life and states a problem that they wish worked on. They then take a sip from the chalice and pass it and the candle to the next person. After everyone has had their turn with cup and candle, any training exercises are worked on, frequently a magical goal for the full moon is discussed, and finally it is time to acknowledge and settle any grievances coven members may have. New moon esbats, at least in my tradition, are mostly practical occasions; think family meeting instead of intricate religious ceremony.

Full Moon Esbats

The full moon is the culmination of psychic power. It is the exact midway point in the lunar cycle, when the sun and moon are opposite each other. This esbat is more formal, as it is a celebration of the moon and the Goddess. In my tradition it is kind of complex, as more than one goddess is honored, but to each their own. In any case, the full moon esbat begins at moonrise (dusk). The celebrants gather together and bannock bread is baked (see Autumn Equinox section of this chapter) and a special potion is brewed in the cauldron. The celebrants call on the goddesses and visualize beams of moonlight being drawn down and filling their third eyes and/or hearts with goddess energy. They pay homage to the goddesses and then call down moonlight into the chalice, which is filled with pure water. The water is then sprinkled around and everyone also takes a sip from this cup. Next, the group joins together to cast a spell for a previously agreed upon goal. Afterward, the esbat meal is held, with everyone having some of the bannock and some of the potion from the cauldron. Finally, any divination or psychic work is engaged in, and then the ceremony is concluded.

Since both the new and full moon esbats are about the moon, the foods and oils, charms, etc. are all moon-related, and so are all grouped together.

Brew

This tea can be brewed during an esbat ceremony and sipped to connect to the lunar energy and promote a relaxed mental state—the ideal frame of mind for magic.

Lunar Tea

>   1 passionflower tea bag
>
>   1 teaspoon lemon juice
>
>   1 tablespoon honey
>
>   2 cups water

Heat the water to boiling, then remove from heat and add the tea bag and lemon juice. Cover and let steep for ten minutes. Pour a cupful and sweeten with honey to taste.

Oil

This esbat oil can be used to anoint the wrists, third eye, and back of the neck to promote psychic ability and a proper ritual mindset.

Esbat Oil

> 1 tablespoon lemon zest
>
> 1 tablespoon lemongrass
>
> 3 bay leaves
>
> ½ cup grape seed oil

Combine the ingredients in a pot and warm over low heat until the air smells lemony. Remove from heat and let cool completely. Once cooled, charge the oil with lunar energy, strain, and bottle.

Oil Spell

This spell is to find a solution when there seems to be no way to make everyone happy. Too many people are under the impression that in order to "win" someone else has to "lose," but with the concept of the Infinity of Solution, all things are possible.

Full Moon Infinity of Solution Spell

> 1 white candle
>
> Esbat Oil
>
> Pin

Scratch the problem into the candle with the pin. Anoint the candle with the oil and charge it with your desire to solve the problem in such a way as to make everybody happy. Do not focus on any way that this might be accomplished. Remember, only focus on the end result in magic and NEVER on the process! Once the candle has been charged, light it and say:

> *Conflict has grown and needs to be cured,*
> *A remedy is sought in which all may find joy.*
> *For good of all, harm to none is ensured,*
> *Infinity of solution, I hereby employ.*

Allow the candle to burn out on its own if it is safe to do so. If not, let it burn for as long as you can and extinguish. Re-light each day until it is completely burned down.

Powder

This powder can be used to ring candles on an esbat altar, and also in spells of purification and protection.

Moon Dust Powder

> 1 tablespoon lemon zest, dried
>
> 1 tablespoon unsweetened coconut flakes, dried
>
> 1 tablespoon cornstarch

Grind and combine the lemon zest and coconut flakes. Add the cornstarch, charge with intent, and bottle for use.

Charm

This charm can be carried to enhance psychic ability. Rub the bag on your third eye daily and before engaging in any divination or psychic work.

Witches' Moon Charm Bag

Piece of lemon peel cut in a
   crescent moon shape and dried

1 teaspoon cloves

2 teaspoons lemongrass

1 teaspoon cucumber seeds

½ teaspoon poppy seeds

1 white charm bag

Combine all the ingredients in the charm bag and seal. Hold the bag in your hands and charge it with lunar energy. Say:

Magic herbs and Witches' moon,
I ask you now for psychic boon.
Let my intuition be unleashed and free,
Empower this charm, so mote it be.

Carry the bag with you as much as possible.

Foods

As previously mentioned, in my tradition bannock bread is a staple for esbats. In modern times, there are many recipes that have evolved for use in the ritual meals. Potatoes, turnips, cabbage, and mushrooms have lunar associations and lemonade, white grape juice, or white wine are ritually appropriate esbat beverages. One of the most well-known foods eaten on esbats are crescent cakes. They are essentially almond cookies that are moon-shaped and a frequent item served during the "Cakes and Wine" ceremony of Sabbats and esbats.

Crescent Cakes

> 1 cup almonds, ground
>
> 1¼ cups flour
>
> ½ cup powdered sugar
>
> ½ cup butter
>
> 1 egg yolk

Mix flour, sugar, and almonds in a large bowl. Cut in butter and egg yolk. Cover the bowl and chill dough for 1 hour. Preheat oven to 350 degrees. Shape the chilled dough into a log and cut off 1-inch thick pieces. Shape the pieces of dough into crescents, or roll out the dough and cut out shapes with a moon-shaped cookie cutter, and set them on a greased cookie sheet. Bake the cookies for 15 to 20 minutes and cool on a wire rack. If desired, you can toss the cookies in additional powdered sugar before serving.

Shopping List

Here is the list of ingredients and items used for esbats.

❑ Almonds	❑ Cornstarch	❑ Grape seed oil
❑ Bay leaves	❑ Cucumber	❑ Lemon
❑ Butter	❑ Eggs	❑ Lemongrass
❑ Candles (white)	❑ Flour	❑ Passionflower tea
❑ Cloth (white)	❑ Honey	❑ Poppy seed
❑ Cloves	❑ Grape juice (white)	❑ Sugar (powdered)
❑ Coconut flakes		

CHAPTER 13

Miscellany

This chapter has listings of nuts, herbs, fruits, and vegetables for you to use in your own spells, rituals, and magical formulas. There are different listings for astrological and planetary herbs as well as herbs grouped by the elements. Every herb listed can be purchased at a supermarket.

Astrological Herbs

These are herbs that are attuned to the different signs of the zodiac. Some herbs have more than one listing, as some signs have more than one ruler.

Aries
Allspice, cloves, fennel seed, peppermint

Taurus
Apple, cardamom, thyme, vanilla

Gemini
Almond, anise, dill, lemongrass, parsley

Cancer
Coconut, lemon, cucumber seeds or peel

Leo
Cinnamon, nutmeg, orange, rosemary

Virgo
Almond, lemon or chocolate mint, dill, fennel seed

Libra
Apple, marjoram/oregano, spearmint, thyme, vanilla

Scorpio
Allspice, basil, cloves, cumin, ginger

Sagittarius
Nutmeg, orange, sage

Capricorn
Sage, black cherry, beet greens

Aquarius
Almond, mace, mint (all types)

Pisces
Anise, catnip, cloves, lemon

Planetary Herbs

These herbs are listed according to their planetary associations. Again, some herbs have more than one listing, as originally Uranus, Neptune, and Pluto were unknown and the magical lore surrounding these heavenly bodies is still being gathered.

Moon

Aloe, cabbage, coconut, cucumber, gourd, grape, lemon, lettuce, mushroom, papaya, peas, peach, pear, poppy seed, potato, turnip

Sun

Bay, cashew, chamomile, chicory, cinnamon, ginseng, hazel nuts, olive, orange, pineapple, rice, rosemary, saffron, sesame, sunflower, tangerine, tea, walnut

Mercury

Almond, bean, brazil nut, caraway, celery, dill, fennel, hazel nuts, lemongrass, mace, marjoram, parsley, pecan, peppermint, pistachio, pomegranate, summer savory

Venus

Alfalfa, apple, apricot, avocado, banana, barley, blackberry, buckwheat, cardamom, cherry, corn, huckleberry, raspberry, spearmint, thyme, vanilla

Mars
Allspice, basil, carrot, chili peppers, coriander, cumin, garlic, ginger, horseradish, leek, mustard, onion, peppermint, radish

Jupiter
Anise, chestnut, clove, fig, maple syrup, nutmeg, sage

Saturn
Beet, black cherry, grapefruit, lettuce, plum, quince, sage

Uranus
Guarana, peppermint

Neptune
Poppy seed, coffee, chamomile

Pluto
Black cohosh, blue cohosh, rye, wild mint

Elemental Grains, Herbs, and Spices
Here are the elemental correspondences for various grains, herbs, and spices.

Fire

Allspice, basil, bay, carrot, cashew, celery, chili peppers, cinnamon, clove, coriander, cumin, curry, dill, fig, flax, fennel, garlic, ginger, ginseng, leek,nutmeg, olive, onion, orange, peppermint, pineapple, pomegranate, radish, rosemary, sesame, shallot, sunflower, tangerine, tea, walnut

Water

Aloe, apple, apricot, avocado, banana, blackberry, cabbage, cardamom, chamomile, cherry, coconut, cucumber, gourds, grape, huckleberry, lemon, lettuce, papaya, passion flower, peach, pear, persimmon, plum, raspberry, spearmint, strawberry, sugar, thyme, tomato, vanilla bean

Air

Almond, anise, bean, brazil nut, caraway, chicory, endive, hazelnut, lemongrass, mace, maple, marjoram, parsley, pecan, pistachio, rice, sage, summer savory

Earth

Alfalfa, barley, beet, buckwheat, corn, oat, peas, potato, quince, rhubarb, rye, turnip, wheat

Bibliography and Suggested Reading

Buckland, Raymond. *The Witch Book*. Canton, MI: Visible Ink Press, 2002.

Cabot, Laurie. *Celebrate the Earth: A Year of Holidays in the Pagan Tradition*. New York: Delta, 1994.

———. *Power of the Witch: The Earth, The Moon and the Magical Path to Enlightenment*. New York: Delta, 1989.

Cunningham, Scott. *The Complete Book of Incense, Oils & Brews*. St. Paul, MN: Llewellyn Publications, 2003.

———. *Cunningham's Encyclopedia of Magical Herbs*. St. Paul, MN: Llewellyn Publications, 2003.

Day, Christian. *The Witches' Book of the Dead*. San Francisco: Weiser Books, 2011.

DeAngeles, Ly. *Witchcraft: Theory and Practice.* St. Paul, MN: Llewellyn Publications, 2000.

Dugan, Ellen. *Herb Magic for Beginners: Down to Earth Enchantments.* St. Paul, MN: Llewellyn Publications, 2006.

Dunwich, Gerina. *Exploring Spellcraft: How to Create and Cast Effective Spells.* Franklin Lakes, NJ: Career Press, 2001.

———. *The Wicca Spellbook: A Witch's Collection of Wiccan Spells, Potions and Recipes.* New York: Citadel Press, 2000.

———. *A Witch's Halloween: A Complete Guide to the Magick, Incantations, Recipes, Spells, and Lore.* Avon, MA: Adams Media, 2007.

Illes, Judika. *Encyclopedia of 5,000 Spells: The Ultimate Reference Book for the Magical Arts.* New York: HarperOne, 2009.

Malbrough, Ray T. *Charms, Spells, and Formulas.* St. Paul, MN: Llewellyn Publications, 2002.

Morrison, Dorothy. *Everyday Magic: Spells and Rituals for Modern Living.* St. Paul, MN: Llewellyn Publications, 2002.

Moura, Ann. *Green Witchcraft: Folk Magic, Fairy Lore, and Herb Craft.* St. Paul, MN: Llewellyn Publications, 2002.

Ornish, Dean. *Eat More, Weigh Less.* New York: HarperCollins, 2001.

Powter, Susan. *Stop the Insanity.* New York: Simon and Schuster, 1993.

Skelton, Robin, and Jean Kozocari. *A Gathering of Ghosts.* Vancouver: D and M Publishers, 1989.

Weinstein, Marion. *Earth Magic: A Dianic Book of Shadows.* New York: Earth Magic Productions, 1994.

GET MORE AT LLEWELLYN.COM

Visit us online to browse hundreds of our books and decks, plus sign up to receive our e-newsletters and exclusive online offers.

- Free tarot readings • Spell-a-Day • Moon phases
- Recipes, spells, and tips • Blogs • Encyclopedia
- Author interviews, articles, and upcoming events

GET SOCIAL WITH LLEWELLYN

Find us on

www.Facebook.com/LlewellynBooks

Follow us on

www.Twitter.com/Llewellynbooks

GET BOOKS AT LLEWELLYN

LLEWELLYN ORDERING INFORMATION

 **Order online:** Visit our website at www.llewellyn.com to select your books and place an order on our secure server.

Order by phone:
- Call toll free within the U.S. at 1-877-NEW-WRLD (1-877-639-9753)
- Call toll free within Canada at 1-866-NEW-WRLD (1-866-639-9753)
- We accept VISA, MasterCard, and American Express

Order by mail:
Send the full price of your order (MN residents add 6.875% sales tax) in U.S. funds, plus postage and handling to: Llewellyn Worldwide, 2143 Wooddale Drive, Woodbury, MN 55125-2989

POSTAGE AND HANDLING:

STANDARD: (U.S. & Canada)
(Please allow 12 business days)
$25.00 and under, add $4.00.
$25.01 and over, FREE SHIPPING.

INTERNATIONAL ORDERS (airmail only):
$16.00 for one book, plus $3.00 for each additional book.

Visit us online for more shipping options.
Prices subject to change.

FREE CATALOG!

To order, call
1-877-
NEW-WRLD
ext. 8236
or visit our
website

⊰ A ⊱
KITCHEN
WITCH'S
cookbook

PATRICIA TELESCO

A Kitchen Witch's Cookbook
Patricia Telesco

Discover the joys of creative kitchen magic! *A Kitchen Witch's Cookbook* is a unique blend of tasty recipes, humor, history and practical magical techniques that will show you how cooking can reflect your spiritual beliefs as well as delightfully appease your hunger!

The first part of this book gives you techniques for preparing and presenting food enriched by magic. The second section is brimming with 346 recipes from around the world—appetizers, salads, beverages, meats, soups, desserts, even "Witches' Dishes"—with ingredients, directions, magical associations, history/lore, and suggested celebrations where you can serve the food. (Blank pages at the end of each section encourage you to record your own treasured recipes.)

A Kitchen Witch's Cookbook makes it clear how ingredients found in any pantry can be transformed into delicious and magical meals for your home and circle, no matter what your path. Let Patricia Telesco shows you how kitchen magic can blend your spiritual beliefs into delectable sustenance for both body and soul!

978-1-56718-707-6, 384 pp., 7 x 10   **$18.95**

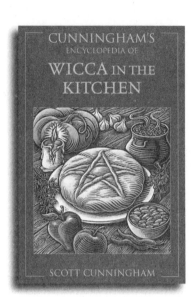

Cunningham's Encyclopedia
of Wicca in the Kitchen
Scott Cunningham

Put the magic back into eating! There's a reason caviar has a reputation as a love food, but a little vanilla or peppermint can work wonders too! You'll savor mushrooms like never before after experiencing their intuitive-raising effects, and a munch of celery will resonate with new meaning as it boosts your sexual desire and psychic awareness.

Change any area of your life when you select food for its magical energy and eat it with a specific goal in mind. This is food magic, and it's served up here in spoonfuls of lore and fact.

978-0-7387-0226-1, 400 pp., 6 x 9   **$18.99**

Crone's Book of Charms & Spells
VALERIE WORTH

Here is a charming little grimoire of magical practices and rituals that reads as if it were written in an earlier century. In a style that is poetic and appealing to the imagination, this book will give you practical directions for carrying out numerous spells, charms, recipes, or rituals—all of which take their inspiration from nature and folklore.

Concoct herb brews for mental vigor and to strengthen passion. Inscribe talismans and amulets to gain wealth, eternal youth, or relief from pain. Practice spells to drive away evil, procure your heart's desire, warm the affections of another, or break a troublesome habit. Conduct twelve symbolic rites to honor the ceremonies of the year.

In a world where nature is so often slighted or ignored, this book serves to heighten your awareness of the magic lying beneath the surface, and the powerful ties that exist between mind and matter, even in modern times.

978-1-56718-811-0, 192 pp., 5³⁄₁₆ x 8   **$11.95**

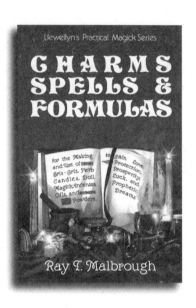

Llewellyn's Practical Magick Series

CHARMS
SPELLS &
FORMULAS

for the Making
and Use of
Gris-Gris, Herb
Candles, Doll
Magick, Incenses,
Oils, and
Powders.

to gain Love,
Protection,
Prosperity,
Luck, and
Prophetic
Dreams

Ray T. Malbrough

Charms, Spells, and Formulas

For the Making and Use of Gris-Gris Bags, Herb Candles, Doll Magick, Incenses, Oils, and Powders

Ray T. Malbrough

Hoodoo magick is a blend of European techniques and the magick brought to the New World by slaves from Africa. Now you can learn the methods which have been used successfully by Hoodoo practitioners for nearly 200 years.

By using the simple materials available in nature, you can bring about the necessary changes to greatly benefit your life and that of your friends. You are given detailed instructions for making and using the "gris-gris" (charm) bags only casually or mysteriously mentioned by other writers. Malbrough not only shows how to make gris-gris bags for health, money, luck, love, and protection from evil and harm, but he also explains how these charms work. He also takes you into the world of doll magick to gain love, success, or prosperity. Complete instructions are given for making the dolls and setting up the ritual.

978-0-87542-501-1, 192 pp., 5¼ x 8 **$10.95**

Magic for Love, Money, & Happiness

White Spells

Ileana Abrev

White Spells

Magic for Love, Money & Happiness

ILEANA ABREV

Each of us is magical simply because we are surrounded by energy. With this energy we have the power to bring good into our lives. Rather than paying someone else to perform a spell for you, you can learn to do it yourself, putting your heart and soul into it like no one else can. The spells in this book are simple and fun to try, and the ingredients are easy to obtain.

Put a few drops of lavender oil in your child's bath and watch him magically drift off to sleep. Take a magical herb bag with you on a job interview. Burn a purple candle to nurture wisdom and family communication. These spells will help you radiate a light that in turn attracts what you want in life, be it health, happiness, or more abundance.

978-0-7387-0081-6, 144 pp., 5³⁄₁₆ x 6   **$9.95**

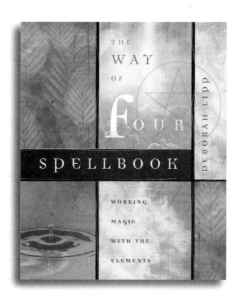

The Way of Four Spellbook
Working Magic with the Elements
Deborah Lipp

Popular Wiccan author and priestess Deborah Lipp is back with *The Way of Four Spellbook,* the companion edition to her successful elemental witchcraft book, The Way of Four.

This knowledgeable guide presents never before explored magical material, such as combining elemental work with elemental purpose in a structured spell. Many different magical methods and styles are covered, including spell structures that are closely aligned with each element—handwritten spells for Air magic, soaking and bathing spells for Water magic, sex magic for the element of Fire, and burial and planting magic for Earth spells.

In her friendly and forthright way, Deborah Lipp gives detailed information on the essence of a spell, including the meaning of intention, the difference between target and goal, the use of interconnection, sources of power, magical focus, and much more.

978-0-7387-0858-4, 288 pp., 7½ x 9⅛   **$16.95**
